GASLIGHTING
RECOVERY WORKBOOK

A Simple Book for Recognizing Manipulation
and Healing from Emotional Abuse and
Toxic, Narcissistic Relationships

Maria Bates
The Mentor Bucket

TABLE OF CONTENTS

INTRODUCTION

"Come on, I didn't say that."

"You're being overly sensitive and thinking things in your head."

"Stop making a big deal out of nothing!"

Do any of these phrases sound familiar? If any of them resonate with you, you may have experienced gaslighting.

If you've had someone call you "crazy" or said you are "too sensitive" for voicing out your opinion, or maybe your recollection of events always gets questioned when you are certain that you are right, you may be a victim of gaslighting.

The topic of "gaslighting" is mostly talked about in a relationship setting. However, it has been reported that many people experience gaslighting at work too.

Have you been in a relationship where your feelings, sanity, and instincts are always questioned?

Perhaps you saw a text message your partner sent to a colleague, and you feel it's inappropriate to send such a message. When you approached your partner about what you saw, they got angry at you for checking their phone and insisted that you were overreacting.

Reliving the message in your head, your instincts are telling you otherwise. But your partner's reaction may make you start second-guessing yourself; you give in to their version, and you go along with what they say.

I've just described a good example of gaslighting in a romantic relationship or marriage.

A partner will use manipulative tactics to control the other individual and make their victim question their reality. When the manipulation persists, the victim starts doubting their beliefs and losing their sense of perception.

Gaslighting is a psychological manipulation that makes you feel isolated, confused, and cognitively impaired.

When a gaslighter uses such hurtful phrases, they try to control you, make you doubt yourself, reduce your self-esteem, and rely on them. The more you remain in the cycle of gaslighting, the more weighed down you will become and the more vulnerable you'll be to gaslighting.

Gaslighting is emotional abuse that can happen to anyone, especially those in romantic relationships. However, it isn't limited to just people in a romantic relationship, as I earlier mentioned. Gaslighting can occur in other relationships, including personal, professional, and workplace relationships.

The gaslighter will try to control the relationship and make you question your sanity. You will start asking yourself if you are actually making up things in your head; you'll question your sanity and feel you are the one at fault, even when you are not.

In fact, the effect of the gaslighter's actions will make it difficult for you (the victim) to leave the abusive relationship because you won't realize what's happening and the effect it is having on you.

Since gaslighting can occur over time and worsen as your relationship with the gaslighter goes on, it is crucial to know the early warning signs to help you know when you are being gaslighted.

After knowing you are being gaslighted in your relationship, what next? What do you do?

First, I want you to know that being gaslighted isn't your fault. It doesn't mean you are a weak individual that will allow anyone to have their way with you. You aren't to be blamed for another person's manipulative tactics. Sadly, many people take the blame for being gaslighted, and they often feel ashamed for allowing someone to control them.

Meanwhile, they forget that gaslighting is a form of emotional manipulation that can occur without their recognizing it. Many people who are being gaslighted have no idea what is happening; it's only when they've broken the chain of manipulation and set themselves free that they realize all that has occurred.

No matter what, I want you to trust your gut. If your gut is telling you that something is wrong, don't overlook that piece of information it's feeding you — something is definitely wrong somewhere. Your feelings are valid, and they are there for a reason. If you can't figure out if you are right or wrong, seek the opinion of others. Get in touch with trusted people in your life and explain the situation to them to better understand what has occurred.

If the signs are clear that you have an unhealthy relationship, you need to remove yourself from the relationship and distance yourself from the gaslighter.

Easy to say, right? I understand how difficult this may be, and I will not downplay it. I will be telling you like it is and giving you all the tips and techniques I used to recover from the manipulation and emotional abuse I experienced.

I'd been in that same situation for many years, and it was quite a challenging time for me. I'd often resolve to leave the relationship, but I failed because I'd completely lost myself and lived like a slave to my partner.

It took quite a lot for me to finally end the relationship and cope with the aftermath of associating with a gaslighter. I can't tell you it was an easy process for me, but every bit of hard work I put into my recovery was totally worth it. The physical, mental, and emotional exhaustion I went through didn't resolve within a day; it took quite some time.

You may be wondering why I am writing this book. The truth is, I've seen many people remaining in an abusive relationship because they can't leave, or they don't know how they could handle the aftermath of leaving, so they would rather stay. This can be traumatizing and lead to drug abuse, depression, and even suicide.

In fact, the World Health Organization (WHO) reported that suicide is the 4th leading cause of death globally, and relationship issues play a huge part in why people take their lives. A study published in *The Journal of Crisis Intervention and Suicide Prevention* revealed that people in unhappy relationships are more likely to commit suicide.

I've been in the shoes of many, and I've been able to set myself free and live a happier and more fulfilled life. I want that for others who are going through a hard time healing from a toxic relationship or emotional abuse.

This thought of what I've been through has been the drive fueling my wish to help people. I've had the opportunity to help a few people around me in battling gaslighting, and they've witnessed a marvelous transformation in their lives. But I was far from where I wanted to be. I wanted to help as many as possible, and the best way to do that was by writing this book.

I want to offer this book to these sufferers as a way out of the emotional damage they are experiencing. The book doesn't just aim at giving you strategies to recover from the effects of gaslighting; I will be taking you through a step-by-step process that you will follow to be in charge of yourself and live a happier life in no time.

Protecting yourself against emotional manipulation can be tricky, especially when you are already in an abusive relationship. However, with the tips and techniques I will be sharing, you can break free from the effects of gaslighting and start your recovery process!

This book is beneficial for people who want to learn how to deal with gaslighting—emotionally vulnerable people who want to escape the shackles of psychologically abusive relationships and those who want to identify when they are being gaslighted and defend themselves against the manipulation.

In this workbook, you will find an easy, step-by-step guide that will help you deal with the effect of gaslighting and defend yourself against under-the-radar manipulation!

In Chapter 1, we'll discuss everything you need to know about the term "gaslighting," the risk factors, and how to spot when you are being gaslighted. Chapter 2 will focus on knowing a gaslighter—their tactics, techniques, and what you can do to spot them. Chapter 3 will discuss gaslighting impacts and how to know when you are in a toxic relationship.

Chapter 4 will show you steps for handling and responding to gaslighters, to avoid losing yourself to them. Chapter 5 will discuss being in an unhealthy relationship and how to break free from it.

In Chapter 6, we will be uncovering the steps you need to take to recover from emotional abuse and manipulation. This chapter will offer you effective techniques and practicable exercises you can engage in to help solidify your knowledge.

In Chapter 7, we'll be building your self-worth and the confidence that has been dampened by the gaslighter. After all that has happened, you will need to find yourself again to live a better life, and that is what the last chapter (Chapter 8) will be focusing on.

You don't need to continue living with the effect of gaslighting; you can break free. When you decide to take the first step, you are one step closer to ending your torment. Fortunately, reading this book is the first step you need to take. It means you want to be healed and live your life how you want it.

You are worthy of love, and you should come first in your life. It won't always be easy but know that there is nothing better than living a life you are in charge of. It makes you blossom, and everything becomes less challenging.

So, are you ready to set yourself free and find healing?

If so, stay with me as we start the first chapter of the book, which will serve as a foundation on which we'll gradually build.

CHAPTER 1: OVERVIEW OF GASLIGHTING

Identity is powerful, and self-perception is one of the most powerful identity tools you can have. This is why a gaslighter focuses their attacks on weakening and destroying their victim's identity. When a person's identity is destroyed, they become more vulnerable to their gaslighters — giving them the chance to manipulate them further and dominate their lives.

Most times, the gaslighting is intentionally done by the gaslighter to exercise supreme control over their victim. Hence, it begins with several manipulative tricks to rid the victim of the ability to restrain control. In this chapter, we will be discussing an overview of gaslighting to give you a better understanding of the concept before we go fully into how to recognize gaslighting and the steps to take for healing.

What is gaslighting?

According to the American Psychological Association (APA), gaslighting is the act of making someone doubt their reality and take on a new reality that doesn't correlate with their personality.

The use of this term can be traced to a UK play from 1938 called "Gas Light." This play was centered on a man who practiced using trickery and manipulation to steal money from his wife and make her feel she was mismanaging her finances, just to clear himself of his responsibility.

After the movie's release, the American Society of Psychology began to pay close attention to the subject and conducted investigative research on the effect of this psychological weapon.

Their research revealed that the psychological term "gaslighting" referred mostly to extreme manipulation by a partner to induce mental illness or prompt the commitment of the victim to a psychiatric institution.

Gaslighting is a mind game used by the manipulator to bring their victim under their absolute control through manipulative instruments including negative words, coercion, self-aberration, and manipulative instincts designed to place the victim in a very vulnerable position by distorting their self-image. It is just as evil and catastrophic as any other relationship abuse that has been recognized over the years. It is usually a conscious effort of the gaslighter against their victim.

Although gaslighting *can* be unintentional, the manipulator is always conscious of their end goal, which is to gain absolute control. Hence, the main focus is to weaken the victim's resolve by prefiltering their every self-perception until it is vague and unrelatable to who they are.

Usually, a gaslighter starts very mildly with small, inconsequential events. It never really appears like abuse at first. For example, when a person is reporting an event, the gaslighter will challenge any piece of information that wasn't clearly presented. The victim will apologize and accept that they are wrong, hence satisfying the gaslighter and giving them a means to further attack or discredit the victim's sanity. The gaslighter repeatedly does this until they have gathered reasonable evidence to make their victim feel unstable and unreliable. The end goal is to manipulate their victim and control them.

Causes of Gaslighting

Just as with every form of abuse, gaslighting is motivated by the obsession with power and control. The only difference here is the gaslighter's approach to satisfying their thirst for power.

You may be wondering why one would fall prey to gaslighting since each person has a mind of their own. The truth is, we need to look at the victim and oppressor's mindsets to understand what's going on.

What makes gaslighting powerful and effective? What are the factors that motivate gaslighting? We will be looking here at three main causes of gaslighting.

Obsession with Control

As mentioned earlier, the end goal of gaslighting is not baseless oppression but mental oppression targeted at gaining control over the victim. Most people feel secure when they have power and control, even in relationships. The motivations of the gaslighter are their interest in power and their obsession with control. There are different rationalizations for this, and they are:

- The belief that being in control is the only way to sustain a relationship: When a negative person with insecurity issues feels like they don't want to lose you, for whatever reason, they tend to gaslight you. Some partners feel the only way to keep the relationship going is to control their partner. So, they apply all kinds of means to gain and sustain control.

- Gaslighters feel better about themselves when in control: Some are insecure and have terribly low self-esteem; hence, they tend to override this feeling by seeking to control that. Who else would be easier to control than someone in a relationship with them? They tend to deal with their own insecurity by transferring it to their partner, so they maintain some form of security by being in control.

- Overly prideful or narcissistic: Some people are just pure narcissists and enjoy the feeling of power and control. They are intoxicated by the mere thought of having someone at their beck and call—doing their bidding and keeping them comfortable by allowing them to take control. They are usually self-centered and dangerous, as they feel they must have someone under their control to be satisfied. They simply and genuinely enjoy having people under their command.

A Closed Relationship

There is no form of abuse without a supporting clause. The gaslighter will need an atmosphere to mix their elements and create their desired effect. This atmosphere, in most instances, is a closed relationship. Gaslighting thrives mostly when it's in secret. If the act is done publicly, others may intervene. This is the case with every abuse—it never thrives in the open. However, when the abuse has lasted a while in secret, the gaslighter may not feel discrete about doing it in public. The victim has a totally new and distorted feeling about themself, so they are not going to feel different depending on where and what the gaslighter is doing.

Gaslighting is damaging because the victim is manipulated without realizing it, except when the danger alarm rings. This alarm can be a simple question of concern by a loved one. However, when the abuse has lasted a long time, the victim sees no reason to leave, as they have come to accept this new perception as their reality.

Gaslighting can be easily detected by people outside the relationship. This is why a closed relationship is a major facilitator of gaslighting.

Overdependency in the Relationship

Sometimes, a relationship might be geared toward gaslighting when one party becomes overly dependent on the other. It makes it easier for the gaslighter to take charge and put the person under their control. Overdependency usually leads to vulnerability. It's like selling yourself to someone for no price. It is important to acknowledge your partner, but you are prone to abuse when you fail to assert your own mind over certain issues. People with low self-esteem tend to fall into this trap. This is why esteem-building is a prerequisite to relationship-building.

Who Is Affected? And the Risk Factors for Gaslighters

Cases of gaslighting are traced mostly to intimate relationships. Intimate relationships are established on trust and affection, making it easy for abuse to occur. Hence, even when something isn't going well, it may take longer for the victim to know. Even if both men and women can experience gaslighting, the APA reveals that women are most prone to be victims of this form of abuse in their relationships.

Usually, the abusive partner frequently insists that the victim is crazy or mentally unstable. They keep calling them names until the victim has no choice but to believe the narrative because of the existence of trust in the relationship. Partners with low self-esteem are most likely to be affected by this.

The attack is mainly to gain supreme control over the victim, after which the gaslighter gives the victim a self-damaging identity to keep them under their control. Gaslighting is usually carried out by the strongest against the weakest in every relationship. In the end, those affected become victims of their partner's control and victims of mental stresses such as trauma, anxiety, and depression. In extreme cases, the victim might eventually lose their mind and be confined to a mental asylum.

Understanding Gaslighting Stages

An intentional gaslighter doesn't just try to manipulate their victim—they break down their strategy into smaller tactics and tricks to successfully carry out their operation and secure their personal objective. These tactics appear in different stages.

There are seven stages of gaslighting in romantic relationships. You'll be well equipped to stand against further abuse or escape toxic relationships when you understand these stages of gaslighting.

Laying the Groundwork

Professional gaslighters don't jump into their behavior overnight, especially when they are narcissists and passionate about taking control and dominating. They are pretty smart in their approach, so they treat you nice at first and over time begin to introduce subtle lies. This goes on for a while, and your self-confidence will start to dissipate. After that, they make you believe that you are unreliable. It is easier for you to believe now because your self-confidence is already out of the way, which is the only thing that can possibly stand up against all their tactics. Then, they begin to insinuate other negative ideas about you.

Rooting and Repeating

The objective of the gaslighter at this stage is to take absolute control of the relationship, so they move on to deepen their roots and make sure there are no barricades to prevent them from taking over their territory, which is your mind. Hence, the gaslighter launches several attacks on your personality by sowing seeds of self-doubt. They reproduce more lies and exaggerations with great frequency, making it look like your perception is blurred.

Escalating the Build-Up

At this point, their acts are already becoming glaring to you, and you are conscious of their effect on you, but the gaslighter isn't done yet. They'll tell more lies and implicate you by creating events that never occurred while denying certain events you both witnessed. Then they begin to blame you for things you didn't do. When you try to react or fight, they will use it against you and make it seem like you are a bad person. Every one of your attempts to fight gives them more grounds to win.

Working Angles Exhaustingly

This stage is mostly carried out by power-thirsty gaslighters who are passionate about making sure they have absolute control. They increase the intensity of their manipulation to wear you down and attack your confidence. They will provoke you into fighting them to tag you as aggressive and unstable. They repeat this process until you are totally worn out and tired of fighting them. At this point, the flames are going up, separating you from your sense of self and making you more vulnerable to their control.

Establishing Co-Dependency

Having placed you under their control, they will make you doubt the reality of yourself, your situation, and the awful treatment you get from them. You will have to rely on the perspective they present to you, live in the reality they've created for you, and grow to become oblivious to real life. You see things only through the lens your partner has made for you. In other words, they make you dependent on them.

Setting Up False Hope

Gaslighters know you can lose your mind if they push you too hard, which is not the goal. It is like pressing a car on until it runs out of fuel or the engine begins to overheat. You are no use to them if you break down, so they try to make you feel safe around them. By being extremely kind, they force you to lose every doubt you have about them and any concept of their awful treatment of you. Seeing this act of kindness will make you start thinking you are mistaken about their acts and intentions toward you. This opens up a softer and deeper part of your heart to them, which can be disastrous, as you only end up giving them more control.

Dominating and Overwhelming

You've lost your self-esteem, sense of individuality, and every form of resistance or opposition toward them in this stage. You believe they are kind, and all that they are doing is for your good. You've come to accept that you are unstable and need your partner to help you maintain stability and sanity; you've accepted that you are inferior to them in every way, and they need to be in control. They set the light and begin to dominate you in a way that serves their purpose and keeps you insecure and perpetually subject to their control.

Finally, I hope you now understand what gaslighting is and how the gaslighter always craves control. In the next chapter, we will be discussing knowing the gaslighter, focusing on the things to look out for to recognize them as a gaslighter.

CHAPTER 2: KNOWING A GASLIGHTER

So far, we've established that gaslighting is a manipulative behavior that entails implanting new memories to make you question your thoughts and second-guess your reality. Now we need to move further along to the next step.

Knowing when you are gaslighted is not always as straightforward as it would seem because the act may start off as subtle and initially make you feel like the gaslighter cares about you, even when they are manipulating you emotionally.

Maybe you've been gaslighted by someone you care about – your friend, the President, or other political figures – and you are unaware of the act or unsure if what you've experienced is gaslighting. Well, we shouldn't leave room for doubt as we will be discussing different ways you can spot a gaslighter when they strike.

Many of us have experienced gaslighting at one point in our lives, making it crucial to learn how to spot the act of gaslighting, shut it down as soon as it strikes, and reduce its effect on our daily lives. If gaslighting is left unaddressed, it can have negative, devastating, and long-term effects on your psychological, emotional, and physical well-being.

Therefore, in this chapter, we'll be exploring different methods you can use to identify a gaslighter and their antics. This way, you can avoid being a victim again.

First, let's quickly look at the different types of gaslighting.

Types of Gaslighting

Gaslighting is a form of psychological brainwashing. The gaslighter uses different manipulation tactics to distract you from truth and reality. The act of gaslighting can manifest differently, but the methods still lead to long-term effects despite their differences.

Gaslighting can make you lose your self-worth and self-esteem and cause mental health conditions such as anxiety, depression, and Post Traumatic Stress Disorder (PTSD). Gaslighting can be noticed in different relationships, such as the ones you have with your romantic partner, friends, family, and co-workers. However, it is mostly seen in romantic relationships, where one partner becomes totally dependent on the other when establishing a view and understanding of things that are happening in their environment.

The following section will explain the different ways gaslighting is observed in our daily lives.

Relationship Gaslighting

This is the most common type of gaslighting. If you are the victim, your abusive partner will make you feel crazy, insane, and less confident in yourself. You will start seeing everything around you from the perspective of the gaslighter and tend to take the blame even when the gaslighter is at fault. The gaslighter will lie to you, try to tear you down, and attempt to separate you from others that you care about.

Political Gaslighting

Political gaslighting is seen in fake promises, false speeches, and politicians' attempts to control the general public's mindset. Politicians will try manipulating people during elections by focusing on just their achievements, no matter how minute they are, and hiding their administration's errors.

Narcissistic Gaslighting

A narcissist usually shows traits such as violent behavior, lack of empathy, and self-obsession, among others.

This type of gaslighting is carried out by a narcissist; however, you should note that a narcissist wouldn't necessarily be a gaslighter.

Child-Parent Gaslighting

Gaslighting can occur within a child-parent relationship. This can happen when your parent tries to control your ideas or beliefs. If you face this kind of gaslighting, your parent will try to mentally and physically assault you and make you believe that you deserve the punishment you are receiving. Your parent may manipulate your reality as a way of making you obey their rules. This act may be harmful to you. Some of the common phrases a gaslighting parent says to their victim are: "You aren't famished; you are just tired and need to sit down." This response may come when the child asks for food or snacks when hungry. The mother is trying to attack the child's reality of the hunger they experience. This can make the child feel they don't know the difference between tiredness and hunger. But the mother could have explained to the child that food will soon be ready or that they will fix something soon, instead of gaslighting the child to believe something else.

Workplace Gaslighting

This gaslighting occurs between an employee and the employer (or their manager). Perhaps you were given a task to submit a report, and you finished it even before the deadline. If your manager calls you after the deadline and asks you to submit the task, you may be left stunned and start questioning your reality, especially when the manager denies ever having received the report. You will be left stunned and think maybe you don't remember anything. If what follows is a bad review and no appreciation for your hard work at the workplace, it can make you start feeling worthless.

Media Gaslighting

This is another form of gaslighting that involves manipulating many people at once. The media will trend something to divert people's attention from their reality to something highly irrelevant.

Note that these examples are not the only forms of gaslighting; there are so many others out there. I've selected just the common forms to discuss, to give you a better idea of what gaslighting looks like in some of its various manifestations.

Traits, Tactics, and Warning Signs of Gaslighters

When you are gaslighted, you will notice that you second-guess your memories, perceptions, and opinions. Most times, you won't even realize what is happening to you. Therefore, you need to know the warning signs to look out for so you can know when you are a victim of gaslighting.

The following are the signs, traits, and tactics of a gaslighter. Even though research on gaslighting has revealed that the act is mostly descriptive, clinical psychologists have recorded a significant number of patients subjected to gaslighting.

Denying

This is the most common sign found among gaslighters. To get their way, they will avoid confrontation and instead go back on their word or fail to agree to what they had promised. Through denial, they also tend to use the silent treatment as a tool.

It's important to observe your partner to discern if, when confronted, they've been denying what they said or did. Has your partner promised not to talk about your friends in a bad light but gone against their word and done it anyway? They may have later denied making such promises to you when you confront them. If this sounds familiar, that can be a sign of gaslighting.

Withholding

A gaslighter may also be withholding by refusing to listen to what you have to say. They will accuse you of being the one bringing in confusion, and they'll pretend they don't understand your perspective or what you are saying.

Lying

The gaslighter will tell you lies, even when it's obvious that they are lying. Their intention is to make you question your reality of events. They want to gain control and avoid the consequences of their behavior by lying and hiding information. When confronted with facts contradicting what they are saying, they will continue lying to cover up the first lie. A cheating partner may deny cheating even when caught in a compromising situation or with incriminating text messages. They may also claim they don't remember doing the things you've accused them of.

Countering

This is when the gaslighter constantly questions your version of events. They will claim things didn't happen as you have imagined and give details that never happened. They say things like, "That's not true; you never remember things correctly."

Projecting Emotionally

The gaslighter will project their shortcomings on you in an attempt to deflect from what you accuse them of. They are projecting if they are constantly lying and accusing you of their wrongdoings. The victim will often defend themselves and be too distracted to realize what is going on — gaslighting.

Diverting

Diverting is another sign of gaslighting that takes place when a gaslighter changes the subject of a topic to shift your attention to something else that is irrelevant. The gaslighter will twist things and accuse you of getting a particular idea from someone else, usually a close friend or family member.

Trivializing

This is when the gaslighter tries to make your feelings and thoughts unimportant. They will accuse you of overreacting and being overly sensitive. This can make you start believing that you've made a drastic decision and sense that your feelings are invalid.

Constantly Apologizing

This isn't what the gaslighter will do but what they will make *you* do. When they gaslight you, you will notice that you constantly apologize to the gaslighter for reacting or having a certain opinion. You may also find yourself apologizing to others for the gaslighter's behavior or apologizing to others unnecessarily since apologizing has become a habit.

Constantly Manipulating

The main goal of a gaslighter is to manipulate you so you'll believe or do what they want. For accomplishing this, they will ensure they leave no stone unturned. They can even use your loved ones or interests against you to get to you. The ultimate idea is to make you do what they want.

If you notice that your partner comes to you with your favorite meal or ice cream every time they want you to agree with them on something, that may be a sign of gaslighting and not just love.

Reeling in Constant Self-Doubt

Wallowing in constant self-doubt can be very damaging. When a person constantly makes you doubt yourself, your abilities, and your talents, that may be a sign of gaslighting. If you look in the mirror countless times before you leave the house or always practice talking before you voice out because you don't know what your partner will say, that's a sign.

Isolating

A gaslighter will always try to isolate you from others. They will try to turn others away from you and disconnect you from people you care about. You will start thinking you shouldn't trust anyone. If this is the case for you, isolation is never the way out. Seek help! Talk to a close friend or counselor about how you feel.

Blaming

This is also another common sign of gaslighting. If every discussion you have with a gaslighter is twisted around to make you receive the blame for what has occurred, that may be a sign. Perhaps you try discussing how their behavior makes you feel; instead of giving you a listening ear and talking about it, they will twist the conversation and manipulate you into thinking that you are at fault.

Questioning your Memory

If in every situation your partner's sequence of events is always different from what you know it to be, and they make you out to be wrong all the time, then the gaslighter is questioning your memory to convince you that you are always at fault.

The effect of gaslighting can lead to depression, anxiety, and PTSD; it can even create chronic psychological stress that can cause damage to your health. Besides knowing the warning signs of gaslighters, knowing their traits and tactics can also help you identify when a gaslighter strikes and be aware that you should avoid them.

Name Calling

Gaslighters will always make you feel they aren't the one with the problem—it's all on you. They will call you ridiculous names by saying you are sensitive, crazy, paranoid, delusional, and overreacting when you express how you feel. They may even inform friends and family that you are emotionally unstable to ensure you don't have any form of support.

Gaslighting Techniques

There are four main techniques gaslighters use to influence and manipulate their victims, and these include:

Technique 1: Reality Manipulation

With this technique, the gaslighter will make you question your reality, and you will start feeling as if you are losing your grip on reality, to the point where you can't recognize what is right or wrong. You will experience this because the gaslighter attacks your ability to accurately judge your surroundings and perception.

Let's look at an example of reality manipulation for better understanding. You went on a dinner date with your partner, then you realized that your partner was flirting with the waiter/waitress. When you questioned your partner about what you noticed and how disrespectful their behavior was, your partner denied it instantly.

Then your partner started blaming you for making up things in your head and accusing you of jealousy and always interpreting things wrongly.

With the example above, your partner has directly attacked your perception of reality. You may start feeling that maybe you've overreacted or that you are being too emotional. In reality, your partner has justified their blame by shifting it onto you.

This technique is very dangerous because the gaslighter isn't even lying about their behavior or character—just attacking your perception of reality. Having this technique used on you can impact your mental health, leading you to question your ability to discern reality.

In the example I just gave, your partner blamed you for always having imaginary stories in your head and inventing things. Studies have revealed that gaslighted victims experience reality manipulation and psychological abuse regularly.

Technique 2: Scapegoating

Scapegoating is when an individual assigns failure or blame to another person as a way of deflecting responsibility or attention away from themselves. A common example of scapegoating in a romantic relationship is when a gaslighter who cheats covertly apportions blame to their partner to justify themselves in their sexual acting out.

Another example is when a gaslighter picks a fight with their partner, and during the argument they get self-righteous and furious, calling their partner a nag and not empathetic. From there, they feel it is okay to act out, and if they eventually act out, it is their partner's fault. Here, the gaslighter will exaggerate their partner's errors in their mind and will use it to justify their cheating behavior.

Scapegoating can also occur when an unfaithful gaslighter blames their partner for not being sexually attractive enough or as good-looking as the cheater prefers. This may be in the form of a criticism of how the partner dresses, looks, and interacts, or it could be basic disapproval of the partner's personality traits. It may look like accusations about their insatiable emotional and relational needs.

For partners that get gaslighted, scapegoating can be very damaging to them while they try sorting out what their responsibilities are in the relationship and what they are not.

No doubt, we all have character flaws and imperfections in our relationships. However, your character flaw or imperfection shouldn't be an excuse for someone to gaslight you. A gaslighter can use scapegoating to take advantage of your determination to be open to receiving feedback from your partner and your willingness to be responsive. This can make you feel confused, and you may take responsibility for things you shouldn't.

Technique 3: The Straight-out Lie

This technique is the least harmful compared to other techniques of gaslighting. But despite its low intensity, it can still damage its victims. The straight-out lie technique is common in romantic relationships and entails the gaslighter lying to their partner. The gaslighter will lie about almost everything, including when they will come home, where they are, what they are doing, and what they spend their money on. This constant lying will create mistrust in the relationship and leave the victim feeling depressed and stunned. The technique is dangerous because the victim usually betrays themself by constantly believing in the deceit, and they will keep falling into the web of lies.

Technique 4: Coercion

The coercion technique entails three phases, which are:

The Charm Offensive: Here, the gaslighter is seen as charming. They will show extra care, love, and involvement in the relationship to make their partner believe that they are loving and caring and would never cheat on them. The technique involves using tactics such as gifting jewelry and sending flowers and other presents to lower their guilt about being a cheating partner. With this charm, they will ensure their partner doesn't suspect anything wrong in the relationship.

Bullying or Violent Behavior: This behavior can greatly impact a relationship. Gaslighters using this technique will yell and threaten their partner with physical harm, sexual abuse, and financial control. If this continues, the victim will avoid raising concerns about their partner's bad behavior due to the fear of physical or mental abuse.

Pressure and Manipulation: Here, the gaslighter will pressure their victim by using verbal and emotional manipulation.

Knowing If You've Been Gaslighted

Gaslighting thrives on the fact that the oppressed are oblivious to the oppression, especially after the second stage of gaslighting has been successful. Therefore, it is important to know if you are being gaslighted. When in a relationship, the following are points to consider to find out if you're being gaslighted:

The other person makes you question your reality

Are you with someone who is always trying to make you feel like you are not sure of what's going on in your life at the moment? No matter how subtle it is, this is one of the major signs and you can catch it early. Gaslighters always want to make you think that your perception of everything around you is warped or blurry.

Are you with someone who is constantly attacking your perception of your feelings, thoughts, people, and situations? You might want to check if you are dealing with a gaslighter because it is usually subtle at first. They will make you feel like you are only imagining things and that some event never happened. This is a general gaslight tactic.

Your partner is always trying to explain everything to you from their own point of view

Initially, it might look like they are trying to communicate their own perception of situations, but eventually, you'll find out that they are trying to pilfer your thought process and get you to think as they want you to. If a gaslighter wants you to feel like you are the reason for your financial instability, they will narrate endless stories of how they were witnesses to you buying things you didn't remember you bought—distorting your mental space and upsetting your mind.

They persistently and passionately lie, even about the little things

A gaslighter set on disorienting your thought process would tell you unnecessary lies about incidents that probably never occurred, to cover up a wrong they had done or make you feel you contributed to an incident that probably never occurred. Sometimes when their lies are not so smooth, you can catch them in the act.

If your partner consistently finds reasons to lie to you and speaks passionately about the little things you can't relate to – making a great effort to present you as an accomplice – you might be dealing with a gaslighter. Even when you have tangible proof and evidence, they still find a way to insist on their lies. The success of gaslighting is in questioning the reality and sanity of a person. Hence, they will question and criticize your account of an event you both witnessed. Other times, they will deny the occurrence of such an incident and twist around whatever supporting proof you have against them.

They always make you see yourself from a negative perspective

Gaslighting is only successful when the gaslighter has control, which is possible only when the victim is vulnerable. Hence, the focus and objective of the abuse are to make you feel vulnerable. One of the fastest ways they achieve that is by presenting you to yourself with a negative lens. You will feel something is wrong with you while they insist on things that would make you doubt your values and yourself. In most cases, they'll try to make you appear like the gaslighter or instigator of the abuse by raising their voice at you provokingly and expecting you to do the same. While you're angry and filled with rage, they keep silent to make it look like you were the one who prompted them to shout at you. They will always try to make you feel like you have some character flaws and are not of sound mind.

They make you feel insecure

Do you have constant feelings of insecurity in your relationship? Another thing that makes a gaslighter's end goal easier is insecurity. It is much easier to control an insecure person than a secure person. Hence, the gaslighter will do everything to bring you to the point where you are dependent on them for most things. They could tell you lies and amplify a wrong you did so you feel incapable of living right. Is your partner consistently criticizing you about a particular thing? You may be experiencing gaslighting.

Your partner always finds a means to alienate you from your loved ones

Gaslighters will always attack your social life, look for who you are chatting with, and limit the number of times you get to mix with people who love you. They tell you to stay away from your loved ones for two major reasons: so they don't get exposed and so you get alienated. The fact is that others outside the mental space you share with your partner can easily see traces of attack and perceive the relationship to be toxic if they get to know the truth. Your partner wouldn't want his egg to be snatched before it matures and breaks into a chick. Also, alienating you from your loved ones is a defense mechanism to turn you against your family — stirring conflict and making you more vulnerable.

No matter the relationship you have or the situation you are in, you need to learn how to identify your partner's gaslighting tricks and act against them soon. Don't wait to gather evidence of direct abuse because these manipulative tricks always appear harmless from the beginning. If you know you are being gaslighted, now is the time to act.

So, the first step toward recovery is to know if you are being gaslighted, and this chapter has done justice to that. Now that you know you've been gaslighted, we'll be moving on to the next chapter, where we'll discuss the stages of toxic relationships and the impact they have on you.

CHAPTER 3: THE IMPACTS AND EFFECTS OF EMOTIONAL ABUSE AND TOXIC RELATIONSHIPS ON VICTIMS

What does a healthy relationship mean to you? Do you feel loved, supported, cared for, and respected in your relationship? Do you feel that no matter the obstacles and challenges you face, you always have a best friend, teammate, and lover to support you and face things with you? When you are in a healthy relationship, it positively impacts both your emotional and physical health. It can increase your lifespan, boost your immunity, and give you a safe place where you can be yourself at all times.

Unfortunately, not everyone gets to enjoy these healthy, ideal, and romantic relationships. While some enjoy healthy relationships, others may find themselves being manipulated in toxic relationships.

Toxic relationships are usually insidious and creep up on you without your even realizing it. Most times, you wouldn't know you are in a toxic relationship until you begin to see the emotional and physical effects manifest. The relationship may start nicely, with excitement and passion, so when it starts becoming toxic, you wouldn't realize it because you are using the memories from the early moments of intense joy and pleasure as your reason for staying, despite things having fallen apart and tilting toward the unhealthy path.

When you are in a toxic relationship, you are always working to get the relationship back to when it was pleasurable and not damaging. It's like an addiction for you; you are trying to recreate the first experience even when it's at the expense of your emotional and physical wellbeing.

The physical effects of being in a toxic relationship include poor nutrition, muscle tightness, disrupted sleep, digestive issues, feeling worn down, fatigue, and immunity issues. The emotional effects are depression, anxiety, low self-esteem, emotional exhaustion, co-dependency, living in fear, and feeling unheard, unseen, and unworthy.

The type of relationship you have plays an important role in your overall wellbeing; therefore, knowing and recognizing when you are in a toxic relationship is crucial.

The next section will discuss how to identify toxic relationships.

Identifying Emotional Abuse

Perhaps you fall madly in love with someone wonderful, and the relationship is going the right way; it looks like everything you have always wanted is coming true with this person. You always want to believe the person you are in a relationship with can do no wrong in your eyes—they will never hurt you and will always want the best for you. Unfortunately, this isn't always true. If you start feeling that your relationship isn't healthy anymore, even when you don't want to admit it, that may be a danger sign warning you against an incoming disaster.

What does it mean to be emotionally abused? Emotional abuse is when nonphysical behaviors are used to isolate, control, criticize, embarrass, manipulate, and frighten you. A relationship can be referred to as emotionally abusive when there is a continual pattern of bullying behaviors and the use of abusive words in a relationship.

Staying in a relationship when you are constantly being abused emotionally can open the doors of negativity in your life. Think of it like a frog in boiling water, which doesn't know the danger it's in. It may not be easy for you to know when you are being abused in your relationship.

If you think you are being abused and you aren't completely sure, I will be guiding you to help you decide if you need to act for the sake of your overall health.

You are emotionally abused if you experience any of the following:

- You are disrespected a lot, and your needs are always left unattended in the relationship
- Your self-esteem is affected
- You feel dejected and depleted for always giving more than you receive
- You are always demeaned, attacked, and misunderstood
- You feel tired, angry, and depressed whenever you try to have a conversation with your partner
- You don't get to be yourself when you are around your partner
- You always bring out undesirable characteristics in each other
- You feel emotionally drained when you spend time with your partner
- You see the need to be careful when you are around your partner because you don't want to receive backlash due to what they may do or say

- All situations are always your fault. Even when wrong, your partner will twist things around to make you seem like the bad person

Identifying emotional abuse can sometimes seem as easy as ticking off the checklist I've just shared. However, it is entirely up to you, who's on the receiving end, to know whether there is abuse in your relationship.

Examples of common determinants of abuse in a relationship are the wielding of power and control, selfishness, unrealistic demands, negativity, demeaning comments and attitude, constant criticism, and unhealthy jealousy.

You can assume any situation that involves toxicity is a combination of both partners' negative emotions and thoughts. Both partners play the role of either the victim or the perpetrator, making the relationship a vicious cycle that will prove difficult to get out of. Due to this, there will be no positive changes; the two parties will stay roped, giving rise to negative results such as gaslighting, narcissism, depression, fear, anxiety, low self-esteem, helplessness, insecurity, and paranoia. The abuser tends to draw up negative behaviors when others are around them and may not even know when they are toxic. However, that doesn't stop the effect of their behavior from showing up in others.

There are many reasons for emotional abuse. In some cases, the abuser doesn't know how to effectively communicate. Sometimes, it may be deliberate. The actions and words they speak are hurtful, rude, and mean. They always make their targets feel they can never measure up to them. If this scenario sounds like the one you are in, it's time to evaluate your situation.

Emotional abuse can make you sick as a result of the stress that you go through. This stress will affect your cardiovascular system, and this is very bad for you.

In the end, know that the negativity in your relationship may bring damage to your health. Think about the undesired coping mechanisms you can develop just to deal with toxicity. These can be excessive drinking, drug abuse, and emotional eating.

If you are going through emotional abuse, repairing what has been destroyed may take time. However, it is possible. Know that there should be no reason for you to suffer for someone else who is feeding off of you. You don't need to believe someone else's opinion about you, especially when it's negative. You need to remove yourself from the situation and start rebuilding your life.

Stages of Toxic Relationships

The toxicity in your relationship may not be a one-time thing. You keep hoping every time will be the last, but you are left feeling like you are going around circles. If you feel like you are going around circles in your relationship, then you are possibly trapped in a cycle of toxic relationships that involves the four stages I will be discussing in this section.

The Build-Up Stage

In this stage, you have observed the toxic behavior of your partner a few times, and maybe you are beginning to realize that it's a pattern. You can now feel the toxicity in the air, and you are walking on eggshells for fear of unleashing mayhem.

You might do your best in a bid to prevent the toxicity from seeping in, and when it happens, you try to calm it. Sometimes, the tension may be unbearable, and you feel helpless. You know something is definitely wrong with the relationship, but you can't pinpoint it. You may have trouble managing your overwhelming feelings, but you still do your best.

The Acting Out Stage

In this stage, the toxicity really comes to life. It can show itself as an explosive situation that keeps happening or anything causing constant break-ups in the relationship. The "acting out" in the relationship depends on what the toxicity is all about. What is tearing the relationship apart? It can be your partner's actions that you can't control, your actions that you aren't willing to admit to, or a combination of both of these situations.

Other "acting out" examples might be jealousy, over-blown disagreements, arguments, passive aggression, loud agreements, cheating, silent treatment, selfish be-haviors, drama, and demeaning remarks.

You are already used to the toxic behavior at this stage, and it keeps getting more harmful. Your partner has failed to change their behavior, and if it's on you to change, you have refused to walk away, leading to more toxicity.

Reconciliation Stage

In this stage, your toxic partner will justify their behav-ior with apologies and actions such as yelling and rant-ing. They will blame you for triggering their toxic be-havior, and after shifting the blame, they apologize. They will start giving you all their love and attention to convince you that you are their true love. They may even work on themselves and try not to act toxic again.

Sometimes, you and your partner may participate in the reconciliation stage because the toxicity has rubbed off you. This will lead to you apologizing to each other. If the apology isn't accepted, the toxic partner will try coaxing you into forgiving them through flowers, gifts, sex, and doing chores at home.

The Calm Stage

This is the last stage of toxicity. The storm seems to have settled at this stage. Amendments have been made, and you both are back to being the kind of couple you were before the incident. Although the toxicity hasn't completely vanished, the relationship seems less toxic now. The relationship seems stable, and you can now walk freely without fear.

Your toxic partner is now back to being themselves as their anger has subsided. Things seem great, and you've become attached to each other even more. Some minor improvements the toxic partner will make may include showing you love and other healthy relationship qualities. However, since this is a cycle of toxicity, the good qualities will diminish as the cycle repeats itself and returns to stage one.

The cycle I've just explained is how toxic relationships work. Despite knowing about this cycle and its workings, getting out of a toxic relationship is not always easy. However, your awareness can help you identify those patterns you are ignoring. Rather than continuing the cycle, you need to step away because of its effects on you.

Impacts and Effects of Emotional Abuse and Toxic Relationships

As humans, it's natural for us to want to connect with those around us and be part of something bigger than us. This idea has made many people desperate to be with someone even if it's the wrong person for them.

The feeling of love can be confusing. Sometimes, a relationship may become toxic without anyone meaning it to, and you may not see the dysfunctional patterns you have with your partner until it becomes too late. This is why it's important to differentiate between healthy and unhealthy before the damage is caused. Now, let's quickly look at the adverse effects a toxic relationship can have on your life if you don't remedy it.

You Start Building High Walls

Encountering bad situations may leave you with a negative experience of something that could've been beautiful. When you are out of a toxic relationship, you will be more guarded when around people and get scared of loosening up because you think the situation may turn out to be just like the one you left. Also, you will find every opportunity to sabotage any relationship that comes your way by finding the smallest of excuses just to leave.

If your relationship is such that you have to endure emotional and physical abuse, an effect you may need to deal with is Post Traumatic Stress Disorder (PTSD). This condition is what makes you want to sabotage your future relationships. You can't overcome PTSD on your own; you will have to see a therapist or use a certain kind of therapy to manage it.

You Become Negative

If you are in a toxic relationship, you will find it difficult to stay happy. You will become used to carrying the burden of sadness around with you and everywhere you go. You never see anything positive in your life and tend to see yourself as a failure, and you are always in a bad mood because of this.

The toxicity in your relationship may eventually rub off on you if you remain in the relationship.

You Can't Differentiate Between a Healthy and Unhealthy Relationship

When in a toxic relationship, your mindset will make you believe the relationship is all you've got and all you will ever get, even if you leave and move into another relationship. You believe you don't deserve better and will never get anything better than what you have at the moment.

Most times, your toxic partner is someone you've loved and trusted completely, so staying in a relationship with them has ruined your idea of what a positive relationship looks like. Staying in a particular setting for a long time will get you so familiar with it that you can no longer tell the difference between a healthy and unhealthy relationship. Because of this, you will easily get attracted to toxic relationships because that's what you know and what you're used to.

Your Health Is at Risk

Earlier, I mentioned that being in a toxic relationship puts your health at risk. Many people may not be aware of this, but being in a toxic relationship can lead to physical and emotional health issues. Toxic relationships can affect your blood sugar and blood pressure levels, weaken your immune system, and cause you to develop a high risk for heart problems. You can also experience fatigue and low energy due to stress and anxiety.

You Become a Pessimist

Even when you are out of a toxic relationship, there will still be a blot on your outlook. You experienced happiness, trust, joy, and optimism when the relationship started. Over time, the feelings were replaced with distrust, fear, loneliness, anxiety, and depression. You will likely carry these feelings with you and suffer from emotional distress even when you have positive things to look forward to.

You will prefer to distance yourself from your loved ones and circle of friends, and you'll avoid engaging in activities you formerly enjoyed.

Your Self-Esteem Gets Destroyed

The kind of relationship you have with others and how they treat you tells a lot about you, and that is an important foundation of your self-image. When in a relationship with a toxic person, it becomes easy to feel bad about yourself. Your partner has constantly denied you the support, love, and reassurance you want, and that's taken a toll on your self-esteem. Eventually, you will lose confidence, have no belief in yourself, and struggle to have a sense of self-worth.

You Become Emotionally Exhausted

Being in a toxic relationship can drain you emotionally because you've spent your time and drained your energy by trying to make your partner happy and fulfill their needs instead of yours. You feel stressed and anxious whenever you spend time with them because they've been gaslighting you and have made everything all about *them*. Because of the pointless drama they suck you into, it is always exhausting being around them.

Your Personal Growth Is Hindered

Being in a toxic relationship can hinder your growth in so many ways. You will stop thinking for yourself because your partner is always controlling and dominating, so you allow them to make you believe you are not good enough to achieve your goals. This can be discouraging, and you wouldn't even want to pursue those dreams. They've tricked you into believing that you are nothing without them.

You feel too emotionally invested to leave despite knowing that being in a toxic relationship isn't a good idea. However, for the sake of your emotional wellbeing and health, you need to understand the effect this has on you. I know admitting this might be difficult for you because it's hard to imagine that the person you love so much doesn't love you back the way you want. Or the idea that they may not be right for you is too scary to think about. But this is something you have to acknowledge if you want to live a peaceful and happy life.

Breaking away from toxic relationships can be difficult, but being aware that you are in one is the first step toward recovery. As you read this book, know that you deserve to be in a relationship where you can be seen, heard, loved, cared for, and respected. I do hope that when you've recognized that you are in a toxic relationship, you take the next step to start the journey of setting yourself free.

Know that you deserve a healthy relationship and can develop good relationship habits. While it is painful to be accountable for a toxic relationship, it should also serve as a beacon of hope for you. Confronting your past will help you build a healthier and happier life.

So what's next? In the next chapter, I will be taking you through a journey on which you will have access to tips that will help you break the cycle of unhealthy relationships.

CHAPTER 4: BREAKING THE CYCLE OF UNHEALTHY RELATIONSHIPS

In the last chapter, we discussed the effect of being in a toxic relationship. Now, we seek solutions by learning how to break the cycle of unhealthy relationships.

Life is all about relationships and connections as we seek to become surrounded by people who love us and care for us. But what do you do when the relationship turns toxic? What happens when you notice that the person you've depended on has become someone else? Do you remain in the relationship and hope that things will get better? The answer should be NO! When your relationship turns toxic and gets riddled with manipulation, there is only one way out—break the cycle and cut yourself off from the relationship.

But before we get into learning how you can do this, let's quickly look at a checklist of common signs you should look out for to help you know you are in a toxic relationship.

Exercise: Checklist of Unhealthy Relationships

What do you look out for to assess the health of your relationship? Mark the box at the end of the statement with ✔ if it's true and ✘ if it's untrue.

- You feel afraid of your partner ☐
- You are controlled and can't express your thoughts and feelings ☐
- You are unhappy and resolved to stay in the relationship because you don't want to be alone ☐ or you don't have a support system ☐
- You always breathe a sigh of relief when the person isn't with you ☐
- You are disrespected ☐
- You feel small, inadequate, and always belittled by your partner ☐
- Your needs are not always met ☐
- You aren't valued ☐
- You give more than you receive ☐
- You aren't free to live your life autonomously ☐
- You are unsupported and always feel attacked ☐
- Your self-esteem and self-worth are deteriorating ☐
- You are anxious and depressed ☐
- You always seem to be walking on eggshells ☐
- Your eating and sleeping patterns have changed ☐
- Your feelings are unimportant ☐

- You feel manipulated ☐
- You bring out the bad qualities you both have ☐
- You feel responsible for making the other person happy ☐
- You are emotionally, physically, mentally, and sexually abused ☐

If most of these statements resonate with you, then that's an indication that you are at a crossroads in your relationship, and it's time to decide whether you want to keep getting yourself involved in toxicity or free yourself to enjoy a peaceful and happy life.

Perhaps, it's time to evaluate the advantage of being in the relationship against the potential effect on your psyche. Your responsibility is to secure your mental and emotional well-being the same way you safeguard your physical health. No one can do it for you.

Exercise: Identifying the Signs of Toxicity in Your Relationship

We can't deny that relationships have their ups and downs, but toxic relationships usually involve a set of unhealthy patterns that can quickly worsen and give rise to physical and emotional abuse. If you've been worried that your relationship might be unhealthy, this quick exercise will help you confirm if your worries are true or not.

Answer Yes or No to the following questions.

Does your partner always attempt to exercise control and power over you? They may be doing this physically and emotionally, perhaps through what they say to you or by controlling your social media platforms.

Does your partner pressure you to send nude photos or intimate messages that you wouldn't want to send? Are you always scared because you aren't sure what they would do with these?

Is your partner controlling you by always dictating how your hair should look, what you should wear, how your general outlook should be, what you can do, and who you can see?

Do you often feel unwilling to communicate with your partner?

Is your partner always dishonest?

_____

Does your partner call you names and always criticize your decisions and choices?

_____

Does your partner make you feel you don't have control over whether you should use contraceptives or not, and you don't feel you can insist on safe practices to avoid diseases?

_____

Does your partner restrict your movement and prevent you from going out with your friends and family?

_____

Does your partner always make you feel guilty about the choices you make?

_____

The second part of the exercise tests your knowledge of unhealthy relationships. The following are questions that prompt you to think about yourself. Share your thoughts in the lines provided.

Do you have a fixed idea about relationships? Perhaps you think there are some set rules for a good and bad relationship?

Do you think your partner should have some qualities that you find in other people? Share some of those qualities you want to see.

Can you tell the difference between a toxic relationship and one that is just going through a difficult patch? Explain how you can tell.

Are there certain behaviors you see that you are sure are not part of a healthy relationship? List them.

How do you think your sexual health can be affected by being in an unhealthy relationship?

What next?

If you've realized that you are in an unhealthy relationship, you may respond this way: You can decide to end the relationship with your toxic partner. This is effective if you've planned a course of action and you have enough support to help you carry out what you've planned. Your decision should also depend on how severe the toxicity is.

To take the bold step of setting yourself free from the relationship, you may need a therapist or counselor to support you in filtering through your goals, options, and motives for making the decision. Resolve any guilt you may have and be convinced that this is what you want to do.

How to Break Unhealthy Patterns

Breaking the cycle of unhealthy relationships can be quite challenging, so I understand if you are hesitant. However, you should know that a relationship that's not building you up positively isn't one you should remain in, and it isn't worth your time. The more you remain in the toxic relationship and ride out the manipulation of your partner, the more difficult it is to break free.

When was the last time you tended a garden? What was your most difficult challenge while caring for the plants? I am guessing it would be the weeds. Weeds always grow where there are plants, and if the weeds are left alone to continue thriving, the garden will eventually look messy. That's exactly how your relationship is. If you want to have a beautiful garden, you need to intentionally pull out the weeds.

The weeds, in your case, are those things that make you feel emotionally bullied and suffocated. Weeding out these unhealthy qualities is what you need to do regularly through assessing your relationships, knowing if you are being gaslighted, and breaking away from the cycle. Your flowers can bloom when the weeds are removed, and the garden will be well nurtured.

This section will discuss maintaining healthy relationships and taking yourself away from unhealthy ones. We'll be starting with your mindset. Your mindset needs to be changed to differentiate healthy from unhealthy.

A Mindset Shift to Successfully Break Free from an Unhealthy Relationship

Albert Einstein has made us understand that it is totally insane to do the same thing repeatedly and expect to see different results. The cycle of toxic relationships can be broken only if you can nurture a loving relationship with yourself first. Without this, you will keep seeing yourself in unhealthy relationships.

Nothing will change if you don't experience change, and your effort will be in vain. To change your mindset, you need to understand this first. Mere wishing that change will happen isn't enough; you have to do something about it to see the change.

In this case, our first aspect of change will be working on your mindset to help you let go of the relationship and be content. Without this kind of change, leaving will be difficult.

The following are important things you need to know to help with your mindset change.

Love Is Different than Obsession

This particular point is very important because it is one of the reasons why manipulation thrives. Love isn't the same as an obsession. Love is when two people have unique identities in addition to their romantic connection. People in love value their time alone and with others such as friends and family. They give each other the support to work on their personal goals and build connections. But when you have a partner who stifles you with obsessive behavior, it's no longer love.

Obsession is when your partner suffocates you, makes you neglect your needs, and prioritizes their needs. This isn't love, and you need to make that clear. The moment you notice obsession has become the norm in your relationship, it's time to take your leave.

You Shouldn't Control Others

This is another mindset change you need to have. Know that you can't control others; it's not in your place and neither is it your job to do so. If you keep trying to control the situation, hoping that your partner will change, you will never break free from the vicious cycle. You can't control your toxic partner, especially the one who sees no wrong in their attitude. Why, then, do you bother?

Since you can't control the other person, you need to decide on being the best version of yourself while preparing to leave the relationship. Own your narrative and rise above the situation you are in.

Sometimes, you may wish for a magic wand that you can wave and get you out of the suffocating relationship. This is just wishful thinking, despite sounding like a good idea. Instead of indulging in this thought, why not free yourself by trying not to control things?

Life Isn't an Emergency

This should be a big one for you! An important mindset change you need to have is knowing that life isn't an emergency. Being in a toxic relationship can make you terrified of people and life itself. You will become worried about everything happening outside of your control, making life a difficult experience.

When you see life as an emergency, you will always be available when your toxic partner calls. You will feel like it's an emergency, and it can't wait. This will only make them manipulate you more. What you should do is t live in the moment and make your needs a priority.

Doing this doesn't mean you are selfish—it means you don't want to make yourself available for your toxic partner to manipulate. Live your life knowing that as you make time for the relationship, you also need to make time for yourself. Don't make your relationship your life. You have a life outside your relationship that you need to embrace. Don't rush your life, and don't allow your toxic partner to make your life feel rushed.

Treat Yourself How You Want to Be Treated

You need to start treating yourself how you want to be treated. Project how you want your partner to treat you. If you keep doing the wrong things to yourself, your partner will treat you the same way, which eventually breeds toxicity.

Trust your mind, think independently, and believe you can get things done yourself. When you need a collaborative experience, you can seek your partner's help rather than suffocating them with your heaps of desires. Trust your instinct, love yourself, be kind to yourself, be a good listener, and don't encourage toxicity in your relationship.

Choose to Be Alone Rather Than in a Dysfunctional Relationship

This may sound like a cliché to you but being alone is a better option. The idea of an unhealthy relationship supports the concept of remaining in a dysfunctional situation rather than leaving. Many people do this because they don't know what people will say about them and how people will react to the news of their relationship coming to an end. Instead of causing you to walk away, these thoughts will make you endure and stay in the relationship. So, you need to be content and choose to be alone rather than endure constant physical and emotional torture.

Tips and Exercises to Help You Break the Cycle of Unhealthy Relationships

Before we start unraveling what you should do if you find yourself in a toxic relationship, it's important to know what the behavior looks like. This will help you quickly identify when you are in the situation you are trying to avoid. Earlier, I shared how you can identify toxicity in an unhealthy relationship and provided a checklist to help you.

The following are tips and exercises you can start doing today to ensure you have a supportive, balanced, and fulfilling relationship with yourself as you break free from the cycle of unhealthy relationships.

Practice Self-Care

I know you've probably heard many times that self-care is important, and you need to prioritize it. But you aren't paying attention, or you don't see the need to practice it, especially since you have a toxic partner.

The truth is, practicing self-care is an important element you can use to break the cycle of unhealthy relationships because it opens your eyes to realize that you are whole and enough for yourself. Practicing self-care will help you tap into yourself and get nourished properly, which in turn empowers your independence. Examples of ideas you can try include meditation, booking a massage session, taking up a hobby, and starting a fitness routine.

Exercise: Self-Care Assessment

This exercise will give you an overview of strategies you can use to practice self-care. After you've completed the assessment, you can move to the next stage, where you can develop a self-care plan for yourself.

You'll use a scale of 4 to 1 to rate a particular area according to its frequency.

4 = Frequently 3 = Occasionally 2= Seldom 1 = Never

Write in the most appropriate number after the sentence.

Psychological Self-Care:

- Journaling ___
- Self-reflection ___
- Reading literature ___
- Being curious ___
- Psychotherapy___
- Allowing others to know a different aspect of you___
- Practicing receiving from your partner ___
- Voicing out when you have extra responsibilities ___

  Listening to your thoughts, beliefs, judgment, feelings, and behavior___

Emotional Self-Care:

- Allowing yourself to cry sometimes ___
- Loving yourself ___
- Spending time with people whose company you enjoy___
- Staying in touch with people that mean a lot to you ___

- Reading your favorite books and watching your favorite movies ___
- Finding things that make you laugh ___
- Reading out affirmations to yourself ___
- Playing with kids ___
- Recognizing and then seeking out comforting people, objects, activities, and places___

Physical Self-Care:

- Eating regularly ___
- Eating healthily ___
- Getting medical attention when needed __
- Exercising regularly ___
- Resting when needed ___
- Getting massages ___
- Wearing clothes you like ___
- Swimming, dancing, running, and walking ___
- Being sexual with yourself or with a partner ___
- Getting enough sleep ___
- Taking mini-vacations ___

Spiritual Self-Care:

- Spending time with nature ___
- Being open to inspiration ___
- Being open to not knowing ___
- Making time for reflection ___

- Finding a connection or community ___
- Being optimistic ___
- Listening to inspirational talks and music ___
- Being aware of the nonmaterial aspect of life ___
- Trying not to always be the expert ___
- Knowing what is meaningful to you ___

The following is the developmental part of the exercise. Write your answers in the lines provided.

1. *What are the self-care habits you are using to cope with your situation?*

_____

_____

_____

_____

_____

_____

_____

2. *What self-care habits would you like to engage in but aren't practicing right now?*

_____

_____

_____

_____

_____

3. *List the challenges preventing you from practicing these habits.*

_____

_____

_____

_____

_____

_____

4. *List the solutions you can come up with to help you address the challenges.*

----

5. Now, read the self-care habits you've listed in question 2. Choose one habit you would like to start practicing and use it to complete this sentence:

I am committing to.... I want to start practicing this because... and I will be accomplishing this by....

Develop Decision-Making Skills

People trapped in toxic relationships usually have trouble making decisions on their own because they are scared of making mistakes or doing something wrong. Due to this, they start losing their confidence and self-worth.

To break free from this behavior, identify those moments when you rely on others to make the decision and look inwardly instead. Think about the situation, decide what you think the best choice should be, and go with your gut. If you eventually find out that you went with the decision that wasn't the best, it's totally fine. You should learn from your mistakes and make better decisions next time.

Exercise: Improving Decision-Making Skills

Sometimes, we don't usually consider all sides of the situation when we want to make significant changes. We tend to do the things we should do just to avoid doing the things we don't like doing. We may even get overwhelmed and confused, and so we give up completely. This is what usually leads to making a poor decision.

This exercise will help you improve your decision-making skills by encouraging you to consider all options and potential consequences before deciding.

Think about the changes you want to make in your life and complete the following steps. In this case, it is about giving up your unhealthy relationship and walking away.

Define the decision you need to make. For example, "I want to leave my unhealthy relationship."

_____

_____

_____

_____

What options or solutions can you use to achieve this goal? For example, "I will put my needs first."

_____

_____

_____

_____

Write the positive things you will achieve and the negative aspect of making the changes, including what might happen if you don't change. For example, Positive: "I will thrive and be happier." Negative: "I will be sad, and my health will be at risk."

Positive:

Negative:

Weigh the positives and the negatives and list the ones that will serve you best.

It's time to decide how and when to implement the decision that suits you best. This will involve creating a plan.

Write a plan that will help you implement this decision.

Write the date when you will be reviewing your progress and assess how you've managed to implement your decisions or if the issue is close to being resolved.

When it's time for you to review, assess how you've stuck to your decision. If it didn't work, be compassionate with yourself and start the process all over. Don't give up—most good things in life usually don't come on the first try.

Cultivate Independence

This can be difficult for you because your toxic partner may not allow you to exercise independence. However, it will eventually make a big difference if you start trying, even in the smallest ways. You might start doing this by seeing a movie on your own, hiking, and dining at a nice restaurant. When you eventually see that you can do things independently and be at peace with your thoughts without distractions, you can rediscover your relationship with yourself.

Exercise: Cultivating Hope

An important aspect of being independent is being hopeful and motivated to bounce back from life's challenges when they happen. Having hope is when you are positive, have an optimistic mind, and expect good things to happen.

In this exercise, you will be completing the following questions to give you an insight into the relationship you have with being hopeful or hopeless. This will help you have a more optimistic frame of mind.

According to Aristotle, "Hope is a waking dream." What does this statement mean to you?

Have your hopes changed before? How have they changed?

List your three biggest aspirations.

1. _____

2. _____

3. _____

How has being hopeful or hopeless influenced your life choices?

What has made you lose hope?

What activities give you hope when you do them?

Where do your hope and hopelessness come from?

How does doing things independently give you more hope or less hope?

What are things that need to happen to make you feel hopeful?

Forgive Yourself

Do you know that you are the architect of your life, and you shouldn't allow anyone to be in charge? Only you have that mantle of leadership over your life. This means that you should forgive yourself for being in an unhealthy relationship. It wasn't your fault — how could you have known that the person who was so nice to you would turn toxic?

It will do you no good to engage in negative self-talk because you feel bad about yourself for being in an unhealthy relationship. Sometimes, you may say things like, *"How did I let this relationship turn out this way?"* While it may be good to ask questions like this, know that holding grudges against yourself isn't ideal.

Now that you've already found yourself in the relationship, you need to forgive yourself and move past it. You are an emotional being that can make mistakes. What's important now is that you've realized your mistakes and want to move past them.

You need positive energy around you now; you need to hold onto your power and keep your hope alive. Forgiveness gives rise to hope. Your subconscious mind may try to control what you do, but you can't move forward if you keep focusing on what your subconscious mind wants.

Exercise: Self-Forgiveness Letter

This self-forgiveness exercise will help you release the negative feelings that hold you back from making the right choice. When you struggle with anger, pain, sadness, and unhappy feelings due to a present or past event, you can try writing a letter of forgiveness.

This is a creative way of practicing self-kindness and self-expression. You can use it to reduce the hurt you feel as you develop a more compassionate relationship with yourself.

Instructions

Sit down in a quiet place and write your letter of self-forgiveness. As you write it, give yourself time to reflect.

This exercise comprises a four-stage approach:

Stage 1: Take Responsibility

You need to take the blame for your actions while being compassionate. Own up to your mistakes and don't make excuses or forward any unnecessary self-criticism. This will help you reduce feelings of regret or guilt.

Stage 2: Showing Remorse

Shame, guilt, and regret can be painful, but these feelings are powerful triggers for your self-growth. By showing remorse, you are conveying empathy to yourself, which will help you to stay more conscious and avoid similar situations in the future.

In the lines below, explain how your past actions have hurt your current self.

Stage 3: Rectifying Mistakes

After acknowledging your remorse, it's time to apologize to yourself. You can do this by sincerely expressing your apologies to yourself in writing.

Write down how you can make amends to your present self for your past actions.

Stage 4: Releasing Past Hurt

You've learned from your past mistakes, which involves understanding the reasons for your actions that are causing you pain.

What actions can you engage in to help you grow from the experience and avoid having the same experience in the future?

Move Forward

You need to take this important step without paying much attention to how lonely you will feel afterward. You need to move forward by stepping away from the unhealthy relationship even if you don't know what happens next.

I know how scary moving forward and exploring other options seems to you. It's normal to feel that way. But know that you are doing this for your ultimate peace and happiness. I encourage you to move forward regardless of your fears. In life, we all have to move past some things, whether we are ready or not. Time won't stop tickling because you are experiencing a difficult situation. You need to get up and get going.

It's better to have a broken relationship than an unhealthy one. You will become optimistic about your future while overcoming the hurdles before you by moving on. Forgive your ex, understand the situation, and know what the toxic traits are to avoid falling into the same trap again. And above all, move forward!

Exercise: Looking Forward

Knowing how your past has formed your present will help you move forward.

Complete the sentences in the following table and write the goals you will work with to create a peaceful, successful, and happy future for yourself.

Past	Future
I thought…	I know…
I was…	I am…
I wanted…	I will…
I needed…	I need…

Goal 1:

_____

_____

_____

_____

Goal 2:

_____

_____

_____

_____

Goal 3:

_____

_____

_____

_____

Finally, many people have, at some point in their lives, experienced an unhealthy relationship. What they decide to do afterward determines whether they will remain unhappy in their relationships or move on to enjoy stability and peace. It's fine to seek professional help if you need to, especially when you've experienced toxicity for a long time.

This chapter introduces the first of many solutions I will be unraveling in this book. Regardless of how long the relationship has been, it's never too late to break free from it and set yourself free. We'll be moving on to Chapter 5, where we'll discuss how to stop being gaslighted.

CHAPTER 5: HOW DO I STOP BEING GASLIGHTED?

When you are in an unhealthy relationship with a gaslighter, you will experience a hard time staying in control of your emotions, and you'll find it difficult to make decisions on your own. You may also struggle with communicating because you value your partner's opinions more than yours.

Right from the first chapter of this book, we've been discussing the concept of gaslighting and how dangerous it is. When you finally know you are in a toxic relationship and are being gaslighted by your partner, what next? How can you stop being gaslighted? You will find the answer in this chapter.

The Manipulative Behavior of Gaslighters

Gaslighting is a manipulating tactic used by emotional abusers to make you question your feelings, judgment, reality, and memories. The insidious nature of this makes it hard for victims to recognize when they are being gaslighted.

An abuser uses gaslighting as their own way of maintaining control and power in a relationship. Your confidence will be targeted, and you will start misinterpreting your version of things and second-guessing yourself over time.

Gaslighting is usually used by abusers who can't correctly argue their point of view. Instead, they will turn to gaslighting to ensure their views are accepted, thereby confusing you. This can be seen as a sign of weakness.

If your partner is a gaslighter, you should know what they can do. They've been using the manipulation technique of distorting obvious facts, events, memories, and substantial evidence to invalidate your experience. Here, the idea is to keep you from disagreeing with them and put your sanity and memory into question.

Gaslighters are manipulators who use false promises, lies, and attacks on your personality to achieve their aim.

Some of the common phrases gaslighters use to carry out their manipulative behavior are:

"You're too sensitive."

They usually use this phrase when you try to express your disappointment and hurt over something they said or did. This can be a hurtful remark they made in front of strangers or your friends about how you look. When you try to bring their attention to what they did, they will attempt to minimize your feelings by insisting that what they said was just a funny joke, you are just being overly sensitive, and you shouldn't make a big deal out of it. Their intention is to ensure your self-esteem is affected, making you feel stupid and hesitant to speak up. Once they can break up your defenses and your ability to trust your perception, you will be more likely to endure, put up with their nasty attitude, and remain in the relationship.

"It never happened."

A gaslighter may say or do something abusive and then manipulate you to believe it never happened. This is to sow seeds of doubt in you, make you start questioning your views, and get you accustomed to the reality they've painted and manipulated for you. This is also to increase your sense of dependency on them.

"You have a bad memory."

Indeed, there are times when we have a lapse when we try to recall details of a particular event or conversation.

This can be normal. However, a gaslighter will try to manipulate you to make you doubt your memory about specific events. Making you question yourself is the core of gaslighting, and when you no longer trust your judgment, you are handing the gaslighter complete control of yourself.

"I think you are crazy, and others know it too."

If a gaslighter keeps manipulating you, over time their lies and attempts to distort your reality will ultimately make you start questioning your sanity. They use this to achieve their manipulative aim because once your confidence has been affected, your worst fear – that you are crazy – will be confirmed.

Your gaslighting partner may also try to manipulate others around you by convincing them that you are mentally unstable. They do this to put you in a bad light and create a distance between you; isolating you from your loved ones. This will reduce your chances of being heard or your stories even believed. The gaslighter is trying to disconnect you from the help you could've used to leave them.

"You should have known I would react that way."

This is an excellent example of a gaslighter shifting their responsibility onto you. They will never take the blame or be responsible for their actions. They will always find a way to pin it on you when they are called out to be accountable for their actions.

By telling you that you should've known better, they've placed the blame on you for speaking up and for how they were forced to react.

"I'm sorry you think I hurt you."

On the surface, this phrase may look like an apology to you, but you should know better right now. Telling you this is their way of not taking responsibility for the pain they've caused you. Instead, they will blame you for misinterpreting them and the situation.

This can lead to you distrusting your reactions and judgment, making you believe you are too irrational or sensitive. You will start relying on their interpretation of things, seeing it as more reasonable and accurate.

Now that you know how manipulative gaslighters are, what next? How can you handle gaslighters when they try to manipulate you?

How to Handle Gaslighters

Despite your awareness and understanding of the term "gaslighting," it may still be difficult for you to navigate and handle gaslighters when you are always at the receiving end. So, let's talk about how you can handle gaslighters and stand firm with your judgment.

Know when you are being gaslighted

I believe you already know that gaslighting is a psychologically manipulative tactic that gaslighters use to make you doubt your memory and reality. Remember how the term was coined? In Chapter 1, we talked about how the word "gaslighting" stems from the title of a 1938 British play, *Gas Light*. In the play, as well as in the 1944 film *Gaslight* based on it, the husband was constantly changing and altering their home environment and would deny doing so afterward when his wife questioned him about the changes she had noticed. He repeatedly told her that she was remembering things wrongly and made her deny her reality even when he intentionally changed their environment.

The common phrases he used were "That never happened," "You are blowing things out of proportion," "You are making it up," and "You are being so dramatic."

To know how to handle gaslighters, you need to figure out when they are trying to manipulate you.

Know the signs too! I've talked about the signs of gaslighting and how you can recognize those signs when you are being gaslighted. When you are constantly gaslighted, you may start experiencing low self-esteem and being emotionally dependent on the gaslighter. During an argument, you may experience a range of emotions, from being confused and angry to being frustrated and finding yourself in a round of arguments, both in your thoughts and out loud. The back-and-forth can be very exhausting and affect how you trust yourself. Once you can recognize when you are being gaslighted, you are a step closer to mastering how to handle the gaslighter.

Be firm in your truth

The aim of a gaslighter is to make you doubt your perception of things. They would rather avoid being accountable for their actions while slowly making you foster an emotional dependence on them. Ultimately, this will give rise to internal confusion, which affects your ability to trust yourself and your memory. To handle this, you have to stand firm in your truth. This means you need to believe in your feelings, yourself, and the truth. You will be owning your perception of the things you've seen, felt, and heard instead of submitting to the assessment of others. You will start using phrases like these often: "I saw it, and I know what I saw" and "You don't tell me how I should feel. This is how I feel."

Don't try to "outsmart" the gaslighter

You don't have anything to prove to a gaslighter who is actively causing you harm. In fact, the best way you can outsmart them is when you disengage totally. Even if you gather all the evidence, recordings, videos, and many more things to make them know you are aware of what they are doing, they will still find a way to deny, deflect, and minimize things. Isn't it better you save your energy for something worthwhile and walk away knowing that your perception remains?

Write things down

If you want to ground yourself in your perception and truth, writing things down as they happen can be very helpful. You can start journaling your experience and later review what you've written. This way, you are documenting what's happening.

A journal is an excellent way to record what has happened over time, and this can make you feel confident about the truth and your view of things.

Grow a thick skin

A common trait among people that have been gaslighted is that they have low self-esteem and self-worth. This makes them very sensitive and prone to constant manipulation. Even at the slightest criticism, they will feel hurt and crushed. This can slowly make them return to the arms of the person gaslighting them.

This is one of the reasons why gaslighting is very unhealthy. To break free, you will need to have a thick skin and learn how to navigate through complicated feelings and events that make you feel uncomfortable. In fact, you need to have a more robust version of yourself.

If you find yourself always relying on your partner to validate your feelings and emotions, you will likely feel disappointed when you don't get the validation you want. Or maybe when you get it, it's not in the way you have expected. This may become a problem for you.

When the situation gets worse in the face of criticism, you will start feeling worthless and unable to protect yourself. Ultimately, you need to have thicker skin to protect you from such an emotional rollercoaster. When it's constructive criticism, you can accept it and work on the areas that need changes. You also need to defend yourself when you know you've been maltreated. You don't need to wait for your friend or family member to stand up for you and validate your feelings and experiences — you can do it yourself.

Don't try to control, fix, or save the relationship

The toxic nature of gaslighting usually feeds off of the false reality of a sense of control. This makes you feel like you know what your partner wants and that it is your responsibility to grant their wishes. Even though it is okay to render help, it can be exhausting when it's excessive. You don't have control over the emotions of others, so you don't need to try fixing them, hoping things will take shape.

When you try to remedy situations, you encourage gaslighting in your relationship even before it happens. You may turn yourself into a "fixer" who wants to control, save, and fix another human. You may want your partner to show you some gratitude for thinking about their needs and fixing them right away, when it's evident that you are overly reactive to fixing everything.

As I said, you can render help to others. It doesn't mean you should stop being compassionate and helpful. However, you should avoid assuming you know your partner's needs before they even voice them.

How to Respond to Gaslighters

If you are wondering how to respond to a gaslighting partner who blames you for everything, here are ideas to try out:

Verify their information privately

Gaslighters are pathological liars, and you can't change that about them because that's what makes them who they are. A gaslighter will lie to your face without thinking twice and then violently react to you when you confront them about it. It's best to verify information privately to avoid making them attack your perception.

Don't argue with them

Gaslighters rationalize perfectly. They use argumentative fallacies and will never allow you to have the last say. There is no good end to arguing with a gaslighter. Imagine a courtroom situation where there are two opposing lawyers and a judge who is neutral on a case. Your situation is nothing like that; it is between you and the experienced liar. You need to deal with your gaslighting partner skillfully and avoid getting into arguments with them.

Ensure the conversation is kept simple

Before you enter a conversation with them, you need to know your purpose. What is your aim? What would you like to achieve? What information do you want to pass across?

You already know that a gaslighter always lies. They actively try to change the narrative and minimize your feelings. So, enter a conversation with them knowing your purpose. This will help you stay grounded on a path instead of drifting in a different direction—one that the gaslighter will want to take you.

Willingly leave the conversation

A gaslighter uses tactics such as minimizing and deflecting to achieve their aim. Therefore, it is crucial to practice self-validation to know when a conversation is unfair and feeling circular. You can leave the conversation when you see the signs of your truth and reality being minimized and denied.

Don't forget that the aim of the gaslighter is to make you doubt your perception. Leaving before the gaslighting gets severe will help to maintain your perception.

Learn to say no!

People that experience gaslighting usually struggle with saying NO to their abuser because they always put the needs of their abuser above theirs. You need to have clear boundaries and politely say no when you know something isn't good for you. You may be scared to say no to your partner because you don't want to upset them or lose the relationship altogether. However, why be in a relationship in which you can't freely express yourself? Saying yes all the time may do more harm than good to your overall health.

If you've had a long and stressful day and you just want to relax after work, do that! If you want to be alone and just have time to think in serenity, do that. You can say NO if you don't want to run errands and do chores at that moment. You don't need to give in to sudden requests just because you don't want to hurt your partner's feelings. You have a duty to yourself before anyone else. People should appreciate the fact that you are putting your needs first. You aren't a terrible person for saying "No." It means you are bold enough to be independent regardless of what others think.

Ground yourself

An important way to handle gaslighters is to keep your individual identity in the relationship. A gaslighter constantly attacks your perception of yourself and the world you've built by using gossip, hints, and doubts to break down your foundations.

Keeping things that matter to you close and protected prevents the gaslighter from manipulating you and having their way. Ensure you always keep yourself grounded.

Assess your personality

It's normal for you to start changing your morals to fit your spouse's needs if you are constantly gaslighted. Be vigilant and don't make any significant compromises merely to keep the relationship with the gaslighter.

Get your friends and family involved

You don't need to divulge your situation to them. However, you need to stay connected with them if things get terrible. People you are close to will notice if you've changed, and they'll draw your attention to the changes.

Rebuild your self-esteem

A gaslighter always aims for your self-esteem. If your self-esteem is broken, you will need to rebuild it gradually and shield yourself from further damage. So, work on your overall self-esteem. I will discuss more on improving your self-worth in Chapter 7.

Be compassionate with yourself

If you've experienced gaslighting for a long time, you will start seeing yourself in a different light. However, you need to treat yourself the way you treat others. Be compassionate to yourself, engage in self-care activities, and be kind to your thoughts. Self-compassion may be what you need to open your eyes to the torture you've been enduring, so you can finally garner up the strength to leave the toxic relationship.

Join support groups

Joining support groups can serve as a safe space for you to be yourself and know that so many others are going through the same pain as you are. You will realize that talking to people who have shared the same experience can help you navigate your situation better.

Meditate

Engaging in meditation will help you become more mindful of your thoughts, and you can even be in charge of your mental health. This is a potent tool for dealing with gaslighting, and if you aren't doing it already, now is the time to start!

Dealing with gaslighting isn't an easy feat. Many people will try their best to save their relationship. However, you need to understand that unless your partner is willing to make the necessary changes and get rid of their toxic traits, you are only wasting your time delaying the inevitable.

Imagine you aren't going through the emotional torture of gaslighting. Beautiful right? We all know how refreshing the idea can be. In this chapter, I've shared with you the impactful steps you can take to help you rise above gaslighting, take charge of your life, and start living a better life. When you finally learn how to deal with gaslighters, you can start rebuilding your life and relationships in healthier ways. The next chapter will discuss the step-by-step process you will take to recover from gaslighting.

CHAPTER 6: STEPS TOWARD RECOVERY

When the road to recovery feels long, soothe yourself and enjoy knowing it will be rewarding. Right now, you are moving from the most challenging phase of your life to happy days with genuine joy and gratitude!

I've often been asked if there is any chance to recover after experiencing gaslighting, and I always give the same answer: YES! Being in an unhealthy relationship doesn't mean you can't recover, find happiness, and still live the life you've always wanted. It also doesn't mean you can't find a light at the end of the tunnel. As with many things, you need to work hard to achieve them.

After experiencing gaslighting, recovery is the goal, and this chapter will take you through the needed steps to attain it. When I say "*Recovery*," I don't want you to just look happy; I want you to feel it and be satisfied with life from the inside out. This is how you can remove any residue of gaslighting from your life.

This chapter will take you through steps and ideas for getting on the road that will lead you to recovery from gaslighting. You will find practical exercises that you can use to solidify what you've learned. Remember to engage in the exercises after completing each step. Also, include them as part of your regular assessments after breaking free from gaslighting.

Ensure that you don't fall back into the toxic cycle

In a bid to regain your freedom from gaslighting, you should never forget sustainability. You may have spent many years in an abusive relationship; now it's time to sustain your happiness to ensure that you enjoy your new life without feeling like you are missing out on things. Right now, you need to reflect on your experience and follow the proper steps to ensure that what you've experienced doesn't repeat itself. This process can be challenging and painful since you've been severely abused and wouldn't want to return to that kind of life anymore.

Look back to your experience and know what you need to avoid. This way, you don't end up moving in cycles. Imagine a baby that is learning about the world for the first time. The baby will surely try out different things to know what hurts and doesn't. When babies touch something hot, they feel the burning sensation and re-coil their tiny hands. That memory will stick, and the next time they see that object, they will avoid it.

See yourself as the new baby that has experienced gas-lighting in the past. Think about that moment when you were hurt and burnt for getting close to something hot. Do you want to get burnt again? You need to avoid the hot object that has only caused damage because your past experience has taught you to avoid such and guard your happiness.

Sometimes, the road may feel overwhelming, and you may think you can't move on from the pain. Remember the place where you were and be grateful you are now out of the woods. Have a good laugh and remind your-self that you can't take the chance of going on that path again!

Exercise 1

What are the pet peeves that have negatively affected you while in the abusive relationship? They should be things that have hindered your happiness.

Write down as many as you can remember.

The next thing is to create a plan that will help you avoid repeating the negative cycles. Your plan should include looking out for those similar behavioral signs in others. These signs should show you if they are gaslighters looking for someone to abuse.

Your plan should look like the following (Add your plans in the empty spaces):

- Protecting your space

- Not giving in to their advances

- Ending the relationship or friendship immediately when you notice toxicity

- ---

- ---

- ---

- ---

- ---

Avoid self-neglect

Neglecting oneself is common among people that have been gaslighted or emotionally abused because they've been made to focus on the abuser and attend to their needs while neglecting theirs. If you continue neglecting yourself, that isn't complete recovery. In this book, one significant thing you've learned is to realize that you are a priority and should put your needs first. With this idea, self-neglect shouldn't be a part of you anymore. When you come first in your life, you can bask in your happiness as you start a new phase of life.

Self-neglect may be birthed by a feeling of trying to please others so unconsciously that you start placing their needs over yours without knowing it. You may think you are just being a good partner, forgetting that whatever can make you ignore your needs isn't positive.

When you neglect yourself, you start feeling like you aren't worthy of love and that the gaslighter is more worthy than you. This leads to sadness.

Do you want to experience that burst of joy that pushes you to face your obstacles with all hope and optimism? This kind of joy comes when you take care of yourself, and you know you will be fine anyway.

Think about babies that are well fed and cared for. They always look happy and bubbly, and they grow to be cute children that people always want to be around. On the other hand, think of children who are neglected and left to care for themselves. They usually grow up to become angry, sad, and toxic adults. Therefore, it's essential to be like well-fed babies. To be like them, you need to be intentional about your "needs" and take care of them. If you can do this, you will be fine.

To start, you need to know if you've neglected your needs. When was the last time you executed your self-care routines? Do you always give in to your people's requests even though you can't fulfill them? Do you celebrate yourself on special occasions such as birthdays, or do you always wait on others? You should know if you aren't taking care of yourself enough and if you are doing self-support right.

Exercise 2

In what ways have you been neglecting yourself?

How do you intend to stop the neglect?

How can you focus more on living a better life?

Engage in things that make you feel free and happy

Engage in exciting activities to make you feel free and start enjoying life. Being gaslighted means you've been living in bondage, and you've given your life, and anything pleasurable about it, to someone else in the belief that they are doing what's best for you. Since you have been out of the situation, it's time to work to pursue your passion as you work on your independence.

It's time to get on with your life and do those things that will set your soul on fire. Allow the happy feeling to be your focal point, and you will realize that you are a happier person when you are awake and doing those things you've always wanted to do.

You may have jobs and business to get on with, but you still need to squeeze out time to pursue your passion, even if it's just a bit. A few moments a day is fine—it will serve as your foundation for healing. Some examples of things you can do are engaging in charity, joining community service, or joining a painting class.

Exercise 3

What activities can you engage in for free and you would enjoy as if you were being paid to do them?

When do you plan to start doing the things you love?

Start living a fulfilling life

When you are fulfilled, you won't need to have regrets or dwell in the past. As you walk toward recovery, you should strive to birth a sense of fulfillment. When you are fulfilled, you are alive and have a sense of purpose that you get to meet daily. You understand where you are now and know what you need to do to get to where you want to be—by doing everything necessary.

Since you've ended the abusive relationship, now is the time to focus on meaningful living. A fulfilling life is self-affirming yet generous, and you mindfully choose how you relate with others.

You can live a fulfilled life if you:

- Start your day by managing and using your time effectively.
- Build meaningful relationships with people that share the same purpose as you.
- Trust your gut and do what is right.

- Stand up for what you believe in, even when everyone around you seems to be following the crowd.
- Set a high standard for how you should live happily and peacefully, regardless of what others think.
- Ensure you are accessible only to those who want the best for you.

Living a fulfilling life can be as simple as seeing others laugh, smile, and express excitement because of you. However, you need to rise above your pain to make that happen. Exert your energy on those things that make you feel alive every day. You can be nice to your neighbor, share your story to motivate others to leave their abusive relationship, volunteer, or start a charity event.

Exercise 4

What things in your life most make you feel fulfilled?

How can you make the things you've listed above a reality?

Acknowledge the unhappy moments

Despite the fact that encouraging positivity at all times is the way to go, you should also know that the bad things that happen to you are part of living. Do you feel like you're in a funk right now? If you do, you don't need to pressure yourself to fake your smiles. It's okay to go through tough times.

Acknowledge your sad moments and allow yourself to experience them for a moment. After experiencing it, move your awareness to what caused the sad feeling and how beautiful it will be when you recover.

What do you think will help you feel better? Taking a long walk? Practicing a breathing exercise? Or talking to someone you feel comfortable with? Know that the sad moment has passed, and even though there won't always be happy moments, it's now time to take care of yourself.

Exercise 5

Describe how you feel right now.

How difficult is it to stay in touch with friends that know you and your ex?

How can you make yourself happy?

Avoid anything that reminds you of the relationship

If you constantly think of your bad experience, your healing will be delayed and won't come easily. You may even go back to the person, thinking you can never live without them. Now is the time to make it easy on yourself by pulling the plug. If possible, avoid anything that will remind you of the abuser—unfollow them on social media, get rid of the pictures you've taken together, delete the conversations you've had, and, if you must, cut yourself off from their friends. This way, you don't have to start looking back at the memories you've created together.

So far, the no-contact rule has been one of the most effective ways to move on and heal. If you know their favorite spots and where they like spending time, avoid going there. Overall, if you want to let go of someone who's preying on you, you need to avoid the places, things, and people that can trigger the feelings you have for them.

Exercise 6

Some examples you can use to avoid reminders of your ex are below. Fill out the empty spaces for other reminders that aren't listed.

- Cancel all subscriptions and gym memberships you share and use together.
- Check your apartment for any reminders of the relationship and trash them. These can be stuffed toys, pictures, and other home accessories.
- Don't go to similar functions.
- If you share the same circle of friends and they are trying to make you get back together, you can politely cut ties with them.

- _____

- _____

- _____

- _____

- _____

Get enough rest

No matter how difficult your experience was, you should never deprive yourself of rest. Aim to get adequate sleep daily as it is important for your health, brain function, and overall emotional well-being. As adults, it's recommended we get about 7 to 8 hours of sleep daily. Your body may be telling you that you need sleep when you feel foggy, and you shouldn't deprive it of the much-needed rest.

If your sleeping routine is messed up, you can do any of the following:

- Keep your bedroom dark when it's time to sleep.
- Keep your bedroom cool and quiet.
- Invest in quality bedding.
- Try sleeping early.
- Take a bath before bedtime.
- Avoid heavy eating or drinking before going to bed.
- Read a book.
- Limit your nap time to 30 minutes.

You can journal the number of hours you sleep daily and explain how you feel after the rest. After tracking your sleep for one week, you should have a better idea of how you feel and if you need to make improvements. If you still have sleep problems after making the necessary changes, you could have a sleeping disorder that needs treatment.

Exercise 7

- Install a sleep app on your phone to help you track your sleep patterns.
- Study the data received on the app, and if you need changes, do the right thing.

Are there any memories or thoughts you have that make it difficult to sleep at night? If there are, write them below.

_____

_____

_____

Would you like to speak to a therapist about it if you have sleep problems?

_____

_____

_____

Be contented

When you are contented, your mood will get a boost, and you will experience an increased feeling of hope and happiness. You can start your day by writing down what you are grateful for. As you continue with your day, take note of the pleasant things happening around you. This can be something as slight as your colleague offering you coffee at work, your neighbor waving at you, and your boss complimenting you on how you look. If you continue to consciously observe, you will become more aware of the positive things happening in your life and then find contentment in them.

Exercise 8

What are the things you are presently enjoying in your life?

What are those things that make you happy and able to draw contentment from?

Look inwardly for your happiness

Henry Van Dyke once said that *happiness is inward and not outward, and so on. It does not depend on what we have but on what we are.* Most times, we try to follow trends on TV or listen to parents and peers to be happy. Buying designer clothes or getting a new car is a quick fix for being unhappy. However, you shouldn't forget that these things won't last forever, and when they aren't there, you will start feeling empty. What's next when this happens? You will start searching for the next trendy thing to follow, even if it's a short-term solution.

You don't need to depend on material things and other people's preoccupations to be happy. What if those things aren't available to you? How then can you remain happy? Be responsible for your happiness by creating it in your life daily. Don't dwell on sad feelings; realize that you are only human and have ups and downs. Acknowledge this and forge ahead.

Be grateful for what you have right now and create a balance with your wants. There is nothing wrong with wanting the good things. However, strive to balance your expectations about your wants and the people you depend on to give you happiness. Know that true happiness comes from within you, and you must encourage yourself to grow, nurture, and develop it.

Exercise 9

What are those non-material things that make you happy without seeking external validation?

_____

_____

_____

_____

_____

_____

Talk to a therapist

Talking to a therapist may be very beneficial when it comes to healing from gaslighting, especially when the abuser has caused significant damage. With a therapist, you can identify the behaviors that have encouraged the abuser to gaslight you, and you can explore the issues from your past that contribute to the present issues you are experiencing.

A therapist can work with you to unravel the issues tied to your emotional imbalance. For example, your self-esteem, confidence, and self-compassion probably need work. The therapist can also help you learn to challenge your negative thoughts and recognize the signs of an unhealthy relationship.

Put yourself out there

I am guessing you've had to shrink yourself to fit into the space created by the gaslighter, and this has made you hide when you should be blossoming. Well, it's never too late to come out of that space. Now that you've gained liberation, it's time to put yourself out there, but only for the right connections.

Go out and meet new people who will add value to your life. Right now, where you are is a steppingstone that will encourage growth and possibly start a healthier relationship. However, it begins with your intentional putting yourself out there.

Don't be scared; it's possible to start a better relationship—one in which you wouldn't have to suffer from abuse. You can give yourself a second chance at love if you feel ready.

Right now, I want you to think of different ways you can put yourself out there. Do you want to go to places you've never been before? Be intentional with your kind of friends? Or build more cordial relationships with people who are just like you?

Exercise 10

This exercise is quite simple. You will be checking off (✓) the idea you want to try out from the examples below. You don't necessarily need to follow through with the ideas here; they are just a few examples shared to inspire you.

This exercise will encourage you to think of new ways to help you put yourself out there with your happiness intact.

- Organize a social event.
- Try out a fun activity with friends.
- Make eye contact and smile when you meet people.
- Make new friends.

- Surround yourself with people who are filled with positive energy.
- Start volunteering.

What other ideas do you want to try out?

You need to have a goal you will be focusing on now that you are out of the toxic relationship. I always tell abuse victims to choose happiness as their goal because it is viable and adds so much value to their lives. With happiness as your goal, you will intentionally achieve it regardless of your past. We'll discuss more on achieving this in the last chapter.

On that note, we've come to the end of this significant chapter. It serves as a roadmap toward recovery from gaslighting, so stick with the ideas provided, make them yours, and stay committed to them. Over time, you will see yourself thriving and winning as you move away from abuse.

CHAPTER 7: REPAIRING THE DAMAGE: KNOWING YOUR SELF-WORTH AND BOOSTING YOUR SELF-ESTEEM

One reason people find themselves stuck in a toxic relationship is that they lack a sense of self-worth, and they experience low self-esteem. They don't appreciate themselves. If you want to recover from this and live a better life, it's important to wake up and appreciate yourself because that will help you take a stand on your independence and freedom from gaslighting.

This chapter discusses the importance of knowing your self-worth, increasing your self-esteem, and understanding how to be compassionate to give space for love and healing in your life. We'll also aim to create a no-negativity zone, which will be the ambiance you will be maintaining from now on. So, let's start!

The Importance of Self-Worth and Self-Esteem

Self-esteem is similar to self-worth and the terms are sometimes confused. While self-worth is having an internal knowledge of being good enough and worthy of love, self-esteem relies on external factors such as using achievements and successes to define one's worth.

When you have healthy self-esteem and value yourself, you will feel secure and treasured. You will build a positive relationship with others and show confidence in your abilities. You will also be open to constructive feedback, learn from it, and improve your shortcomings.

With healthy self-esteem and self-worth, you will:

- Be confident in your ability to make timely decisions
- Be assertive in experiencing your view and needs
- Have realistic expectations and not be overcritical of yourself
- Build healthy and honest relationships
- Be more resilient and able to overcome stress and obstacles

To have a healthy view of yourself doesn't mean you should blow your own horn—it's about respecting and loving yourself amid your flaws.

How to Boost Your Self-Esteem and Increase Your Self-Worth

The following are ways to boost your sense of self-worth and self-esteem. These ideas aim at ensuring that you will start valuing yourself and love and respect yourself regardless of what you find.

Know that you are never a mistake

Yes, you aren't a mistake! Perhaps you've been made to believe so many wrong things about yourself, including that you can never amount to anything, you aren't worthy of more love, and you can't get things done on your own. However, you need to know that you are a whole and an amazing person who is set on achieving a lot, and you need to believe in yourself to achieve those things.

Regardless of what people may say about you, never forget how blessed and unique you are; everything you need to thrive is in you. But first, you need to have that belief and hold onto it until it becomes natural to you.

You are never a mistake, you aren't clumsy or sloppy, and neither are you a parasite feeding on others. It's time to get out of your way and forget the lies and hurtful words the gaslighter has used on you. Keeping them in your mind will do more harm than good, so you need to get the counter-narratives out of your head and begin to feed on positive vibes only.

It's never too late to get out of the negativity bubble you are in, and I am glad that an important objective of this book is to ensure that you get to the pinnacle of positivity, which will set you free from toxicity and further set you on the right path.

Exercise: Challenging negative thoughts

This exercise aims at challenging your thoughts with critical thinking.

Use the example below to answer the questions.

Example

The Negative Thought

> I can never be good enough.

What is the substantial evidence supporting the thought?

> - My ex always makes me feel that way
> - My ex told me that

Is there any evidence contrary to my thought?

> - I haven't tried to prove my partner wrong
> - I believe in others more than myself

Am I interpreting the situation without considering all the evidence?

> Yes, because I am not giving myself a chance to prove my ex wrong. I am basing my judgment on assumptions.

What would a friend do in this situation?

> Probably do the right thing by giving themselves a chance.

Your turn:

The Negative Thought

What is the substantial evidence supporting the thought?

Is there any evidence contrary to my thought?

Am I interpreting the situation without considering all the evidence?

What would a friend do in this situation?

You aren't what your ex says you are

When your abuser becomes your ex, you may still struggle to move forward, especially when the abuser has used many hurtful words on you. These words have significantly affected your self-worth and confidence. But do you know that the words have more influence when you keep them in your heart? You may even start believing them over time.

Allow the pain you are feeling to go away along with your past relationship. Those words aren't a reflection of who you are, and you are already in your new reality. Focus on that.

When the abuser notices you want to walk away, they may use hurtful words to tear you down even more by saying things like, "You will never amount to anything," "You can't do without me," and "No one will value you." Words like these can make you feel that staying in the relationship may be your best bet. Thankfully, you know now that independence is your best bet, and that's what we are striving to achieve. Right now, you are on your way to living the best years of your life as you leave the relationship.

Exercise: Positive self-talk

How you see and talk to yourself matters. You need to change those negative narratives to positive ones. Use the examples below to fill out your positive and negative narratives.

- *Negative narrative:*

  I am too ugly to go out.

  Positive narrative:

  I am beautiful in and out; I radiate everything good.

- *Negative narrative:*

  I have no skills and won't be able to get a job.

  Positive narrative:

  I can always develop my skills and master anything I set my mind on.

- *Negative narrative:*

  No one likes me.

  Positive narrative:

  Maybe my ex doesn't, but that isn't everybody.

Your turn:

- *Negative narrative:*

  _____

  _____

- *Positive narrative:*

  _____

  _____

- *Negative narrative:*

  _____

  _____

- *Positive narrative:*

Be compassionate

You need to be kind to people because how you treat them will reflect how you want to be treated. You can start making people – especially those that have had a similar experience to yours – feel valued, loved, appreciated, and wanted because you've experienced how not having any of those feels. Be nice to people, encourage them, cheer them on, and make them believe in the idea of independence and not remaining in an unhealthy relationship.

Compassion can improve your self-worth. By being kind, you are uplifting your spirit and improving your self-esteem. However, it is important that you don't start people-pleasing, thinking you are trying to be compassionate.

People-pleasing makes you prone to being used and taken advantage of. This might even cause more harm to your self-esteem. Differentiate kindness from people-pleasing and don't engage in the latter.

Exercise: Practicing self-compassion

This exercise seeks to bring you awareness of how you treat people by answering the following questions.

Think about when a friend is struggling and feels bad about themselves. Write down how you would respond to your friend in this situation. What would you say or do, noting the tone used?

_____

_____

_____

_____

Think about those times you were struggling or felt bad about yourself. How did you respond to yourself? Write what you normally do or say, noting the tone you used.

_____

_____

_____

_____

Did you notice any difference in the tone? If you did, what made you treat yourself differently from others?

How do you think things would change if you respond to yourself the same way you respond to a struggling friend?

When are you going to start treating yourself better?

Be assertive

Gaslighting can affect your sense of self-worth because you've been made to feel like you don't have a voice or a choice. You've been made to believe the lies that say you can't stand on your own and need to depend on your abuser for things. You start thinking you will fail if you attempt doing things on your own.

By being assertive, you show confidence in the choice you make independently, and you can navigate through life without relying on others. Assertiveness here goes beyond the context of being vocal with others; it is also about being open and true to yourself.

You need to start telling yourself the truth and mind what you say to yourself. Assertiveness should start with you. When you are assertive with yourself, people can't dictate how you should live your life or have a hold over you.

Assertiveness can help you rebuild your self-worth by saying what you need to say—expressing yourself and not holding back. When you first become assertive, people may not understand this new aspect of you. Over time, they will adjust and accept the new and better version of you.

If you feel like you are being too forward in expressing your feelings, the effect gaslighting has had on you is at play, and you need to break free from the shackles.

Don't cower in fear over what people may think or say—you are only trying to regain your confidence while ensuring you are not put down. When you find your voice, people will start appreciating you, respecting you, and treating you better. Right now, they need to know that you are ready for your freedom and independence, and you are no longer getting yourself involved in a relationship that adds no value to you.

You can achieve so much by being assertive, and if you've been dimming your light to make others shine, now is the time to come out and be the star that you were born to be.

Exercise: Being assertive

In this exercise, you will recall a scenario where you were assertive in communication. In each scenario, write the emotions you felt. Use the provided example in scenario 1 to complete scenarios 2 and 3.

Scenario 1:

A colleague called you and asked if you could assist with a task given to him. You responded: *"I would've loved to help, but I am equally busy with my task and need to focus on it."*

The emotions you felt

Empowered, calm, and relieved.

Scenario 2:

_____

_____

_____

The emotions you felt

_____

_____

_____

Scenario 3:

_____

_____

_____

The emotions you felt

Your dress should reflect how you want to feel inside

You may be thinking, *"What does the way I dress have to do with my self-worth and confidence?"* People who don't pay attention to what they wear and how they look are not very conscious of their self-worth. If you've been gaslighted into dressing a certain way to grant the wishes of your abuser, now is the time to burst forth and shine. Ensure that this reflects on how you appear. Stop dressing like a hag or a hobo, take care of your messy hair or maybe get a flattering haircut, stay well-groomed, and do a wardrobe overhaul.

Dress how you want people to address you; the impression you give to others matters. If you want to be respected as an independent person, then you need to look the part. Be well dressed, and people will start taking you seriously.

When you dress well, you will feel more confident about life. You get this natural feeling when you look good; you will feel you don't need to depend on anyone to have a better life. That is a positive energy that is useful for recovery. Always show up looking ready!

Use positive affirmations

Since self-worth depends on feeling good about yourself, reciting positive self-affirmations can help you feel less stressed, less dependent on people, and more empowered instead.

Building your self-worth is like building a house—you need to have a solid foundation. We'll be using affirmations as a strong foundation on which you can build your tower. Many successful people have revealed the power of affirmations in their lives and how it has affected them positively.

What words do you speak to yourself? Do you always say, *"I am so damned, I am confused, and don't know how to handle life?"* If that sounds like you, you will always feel demotivated. You need to change how you speak to yourself by using only positive words.

With affirmations, you can replace those negative thoughts with positive ones. Affirmations harness the power of your mind and direct your intentions to the best aspect of yourself. It lowers your body's stress levels, which have been triggered by the abuse you've experienced.

Exercise: Practicing positive affirmations

Your affirmations should be positively focused to have a healthy impact on your self-esteem. The exercise below aims at helping you create your own affirmations — ones which resonate with you best. Practice them regularly, and it will help enhance your self-esteem over time.

Example:

1. I value myself
2. I deserve everything good
3. I am thankful for my past and know my future is bright
4. I am worthy of love
5. I am an embodiment of strength, wealth, and beauty

Your turn:

Write 5 positive affirmations you can say to yourself.

1. _____

_____

2. _____

_____

3. _____

   _____

4. _____

   _____

5. _____

   _____

Understand, accept, and appreciate yourself

Another way you can build your self-esteem is to know who you are, accept that, and appreciate yourself. When you have self-worth, you know you have flaws and sometimes do what you shouldn't be doing. You also know that you are only human because of this, which doesn't stop you from being awesome.

Let me break it down for a better understanding.

Understand: Who are you? What were you like before the unhealthy relationship? Who do you see yourself as? Is it that you didn't have a chance to make yourself healthy because you didn't know yourself? You need to know yourself and find out exactly who you are.

Accept: It's time to practice accepting yourself. You now know who you are, but do you accept the original version of yourself? Do you appreciate your wins, values, and strengths? By accepting yourself, you are conscious of who you are without any form of judgment. This is a great starting point for your new life.

Appreciate: Now, you need to appreciate who you are and love all of you. Appreciation here means you see yourself and value your abilities. With this mindset, you can influence others to appreciate you too. You can appreciate yourself by giving yourself a nice treat, saying lovely things to yourself, writing a love letter to yourself, or giving yourself a high five or a pat on the back.

Exercise: Identifying your qualities

Fill in the following lines with at least three responses to each of the statements.

The things I am good at are:

I've been of help to others by:

_____

_____

_____

_____

I love my appearance because:

_____

_____

_____

_____

What I value the most are:

_____

_____

_____

_____

The obstacles I have overcome are:

I've received these compliments:

What makes me unique is:

I've made others happy when:

Create a No-Negativity Zone in Your Life

We've established that self-worth is all about having a positive mindset about yourself. This is what opens the door to being accepted, confident, bold, and faithful in your abilities to succeed regardless of what comes your way. To build your self-worth after being gaslighted for a long time, you need to create a space for the "no-negativity" zone in your life. People won't have access to this space and can't disrupt the positivity in you.

Creating a no-negativity zone means creating a life overflowing with positivity, from how you feel about yourself to how you interact with people. You know your flaws and know they don't stop you from celebrating your wins, successes, and strength.

When you build a no-negativity fortress, it becomes difficult for any gaslighter to penetrate. You are in a state where you believe in yourself and your abilities to progress independently.

You may be wondering how to do this. You can start by believing the best things about yourself and allow only positive words around you. Don't use negative words and don't allow other people to use them around you. Make everyone around you feel loved and appreciated. Share what you've learned about growth with them.

Strive to show up every day to win, look confident, and know what you can offer. Soon, people will see the positive things about you and will, in turn, boost your confidence when you feel seen and appreciated.

Think about the quality of your life. Do you believe you can succeed if you break free from the chains of gaslighting? Does your life seem uplifting to you? If you aren't sure of the answers, you need to change your mindset to ensure there is an overflow of positive energy around you. This will undoubtedly improve your sense of self-worth.

When you have your self-worth at the level you want it to be, you are one step closer to your healing. At this level, you need to find your happiness again. Head over to the final chapter of this book, where you will have access to steps for gaining back your happiness after recovery.

CHAPTER 8: YOUR ROAD TO HAPPINESS AFTER RECOVERY

The last chapter discussed how to recognize your self-worth and boost your self-esteem. This chapter will be the final lap of your learning, as it will take you through steps you can take to get you on the road to happiness after experiencing abuse. You will realize the difference in your life after stepping away from the shadows of gaslighting and into a new world.

Ensure that you are happy in everything you do. Happiness gives meaning to life. No doubt, you are experiencing a whirlwind of emotions right now, and getting lost in it is easy. However, you must find your happiness again—it completes your recovery process. When you are happy, you will realize that despite the few hurtful lessons life may have taught you, that shouldn't stop you from using the experience to become better.

What you need for your happiness is explained here in easy-to-follow steps. This serves as a practical guide to finding your happiness. Are you ready for this exciting chapter? Let's start!

Set Realistic Expectations

You need time to heal and get back to your bubbly self. More importantly, you need to be patient with your recovery process. You can't just wave a magic wand and expect everything to go back to how it was before the abuse. I wish I could tell you everything will be fine in a few days but the sad part is that recovery varies for everyone.

When you set realistic expectations, you are honest with your pain, knowing that you will be happy again. You don't need to rush it, and you shouldn't stall it either. Be conscious of your feelings and emotions daily. When you realize that going back to the abuser isn't an option to consider, you are slowly getting to where you should be.

Take Your Time

The idea of regaining happiness may seem like something that will happen immediately after leaving the abuser. This has made people pressure themselves to find their happiness, and they eventually become frustrated. You are in your recovery phase, so take your time, and you will be happy again. However, you need to figure out where you want to be, where you are right now, and where you are coming from.

Don't Suppress the Feelings

This is another great tip. Your emotions may be overwhelming sometimes, and you may feel like suppressing them to feel better. The truth is, you shouldn't be doing that because you may have to go through the pain all over again. Allow your emotions to find their expression, dig into them, and release them.

Pick Yourself Up

To be happy again, you need to pick yourself up from where you've been made to hide. Overcome those thoughts in your head telling you that there is nothing good ahead of you and that you shouldn't bother trying.

Now is the time to get rid of those thoughts and move from the point you are in. Why do you need to stay stagnant, filling your head with thoughts such as *"There is nothing for me again"* or *"I don't know where to go"* when you should be looking around the maze and working toward the new life waiting ahead. Some days, you may feel like you are moving too fast, and other days, you may feel like you aren't moving at all. The important thing here is that there is progress.

Take a Break from Social Media

If everything feels too overwhelming, maybe it's time to take a break from social media. You have time to do all that later, but you need to focus on cultivating happiness for now. Of course, social media isn't the problem, but your situation right now is sensitive. You shouldn't be on a platform where some people display toxicity. Social media gives the impression that toxicity is fine (people bullying each other), and you don't need that connection now.

Social media may remind you of your ex, especially if it's a space you both used together. Right now, you are creating an independent life that is filled with positive energy. Don't allow social media to influence your decisions so that you start getting reminders of your past.

Practicing "Smart Selfishness"

Now that you want to cultivate happiness, you need to start putting yourself before anyone else. Permit me to call this being smartly selfish with your time and effort. This will ensure that you stay on track and not veer off your path to happiness.

You can practice this by granting your wishes, wants, and feelings. Book a spa session, go see a movie, visit the gym, take dance classes, and do yoga. There are so many things you can do to spur your satisfaction.

Create a Plan

When you were in an unhealthy relationship, you had no choice but to heed whatever your abuser said and cower in fear. Now that you are out, it's time to design a ritual that supports your happiness. Your ritual should include what you like doing or would like to do.

Morning Rituals

- Wake up and say a prayer for guidance throughout your day
- Eat a healthy breakfast
- Journal
- Make your bed and ensure it's clean and tidy
- Enjoy a warm cup of coffee
- Meditate
- Smile

Evening Rituals

- Shower with warm water
- Wear comfortable sleepwear
- Declutter and maintain a clean space
- Read a book
- Watch television
- Sleep for long hours

Don't Let This Affect the Other Aspects of Your Life

It's important that you don't allow the breakup from your ex to affect other aspects of your life. No doubt, this is a challenging phase, but hey! You need to build your happiness. It will be better if you don't compromise it by allowing your experience to affect your zeal to get a job, start a business, or work toward a promotion.

Don't allow the break-up, which was essential for your happiness, to find its way back to you and affect your healing process. If you allow that, you won't have a foundation on which to build your happy life.

Practice Clear and Direct Communication

Communicating clearly and directly will help you get your message across the way you want. Clearly communicate your disappointments, needs, and other things that concern your life so that you can't help but stick to your rules. Be clear on who you are — you've been quiet for too long in the shadows, and now it's time to be and do you!

Find Healthier Alternatives to Unhealthy Ones

Don't tolerate any form of toxicity around you because you are just getting out of one situation, and you shouldn't revert to your prior experience. Find healthier alternatives and ensure the path to your happiness is free from the old patterns that once roped you into toxic relationships.

Finally, we have to come to the end of this chapter. I am excited knowing that you will be achieving a lot after this. I believe you can redefine what survival means to you from whatever wanted to break you. Before I go, there is a final part of the book I want you to read; it will serve as a wake-up call to practice what you've learned so far.

FINAL WORDS

Good job!

Now that we're at the end of this book, I must commend you for doing a great reading job to get to this moment. I believe it's been exciting for you the way it has been for me, and I can't wait to see you doing great things out there.

We all want to live a life without stress—one that is free of pain and the burden of emotional manipulation. However, do you think just desiring this without actually working for it will get you any closer to your wishes? So far, I've talked about the need to be intentional with what you want and that you need to always evaluate the relationships you build, ignoring the temptation of going back to your abusive ex.

I've always had a passion for this topic because I understand the pain that comes with being abused. I am happy to have this opportunity to share my effective plan, which has liberated many people who were in the same rut as you. I am sharing this book as my special gift to you to give you hope that you can actually heal from the abuse and manipulation you've experienced.

We started this journey with a foundational chapter where we discussed the meaning of gaslighting, explored its causes and risk factors, and came to an understanding of the different stages of gaslighting.

Chapter 2 focused on figuring out who a gaslighter is. To know this, we discussed the different types of gaslighters and the behaviors, warning signs, and tactics gaslighters use on their victim to manipulate them.

Chapter 3 highlighted the impact and effect that being in a toxic relationship has on victims. While some may know when they are in a toxic relationship, others may not realize it. Therefore, the signs to look out for were outlined. Also, a step-by-step process to break free from an unhealthy relationship was shared.

Then we moved on to Chapter 4, where we discussed how to break the cycle of an unhealthy relationship. This chapter, with practical sections, gave insight into breaking the cycle of a dysfunctional relationship.

Chapter 5 answered the question, "How do I stop being gaslighted?" We examined the manipulative behavior of gaslighters, and the different ways to handle gaslighters were emphasized. Then we discussed how to respond to gaslighters while focusing on building a healthy relationship with yourself.

Many healthy steps to healing yourself after being emotionally manipulated were discussed in Chapter 6. There are practical exercises in this chapter you should engage in. Continue practicing them even after reading this book — the benefits await you.

Knowing your self-worth and improving your self-esteem is an important step to help you recover from abuse. The importance of building on these two features was discussed in Chapter 7. You are a unique being — important and special. Those hurtful things your ex said to you shouldn't be used to describe you, so be kind to yourself and create a space for healing instead. Breaking free from a toxic relationship is definitely not the end of the world — don't become tainted in how you see yourself.

When I was putting this book together, I wanted it to have a compact guide with everything you need to cultivate happiness after being emotionally damaged. In Chapter 8, the last chapter, we discussed how to make yourself happy despite the odds. We discussed some necessary changes you need to make to allow a positive change in your life, including leaving social media, not suppressing your feelings, and setting realistic expectations, among others.

To see results, you need to start executing everything you've read in this book. Just knowing there's something that can potentially turn things around and change your life isn't enough; you need to implement what you've learned. Implementing it means you try to utilize what you've gained to add value to your life. Don't abandon this book and the information in it after you're done reading. Always revisit the strategies outlined in the book and apply them to the situation as you see fit.

Are you ready to launch into a new phase of your life, where you will experience freedom from nurturing abuse in your relationships? Right now, you are equipped with all you need to thrive and live a happier and more fulfilled life. You just need to implement the ideas that I've shared, and you will see your healing coming sooner than expected.

Finally, I hope this book changes your life positively.

Best wishes!

DOWNLOADABLE WORKSHEETS

Please go to the below URL to download all worksheets (in pdf format) given in the book.

Https://TheMentorBucket.Com/grw_ws.pdf

www.ingramcontent.com/pod-product-compliance
Lightning Source LLC
Chambersburg PA
CBHW031528120626
46545CB00005B/2047